## Houghton Mifflin Harcourt

**ALGEBRA 2 TEACHER GUIDE**

# Common Core Assessment Readiness

Printed in the U.S.A.

ISBN 978-0-547-87714-3

8 10 0299 22 21 20 19 18 17 16 15

4500652413 BCDEFG

Printed in the U.S.A.

ISBN   978-0-547-87714-3
8 9 10   2266   22 21 20 19 18 17 16 15
4500552413   B C D E F G

# Contents

## Number and Quantity

### The Real Number System

### Quantities

### The Complex Number System

## Algebra

### Seeing Structure in Expressions

---

## Reasoning with Equations and Inequalities

# Functions

## Interpreting Functions

**Interpret functions that arise in applications in terms of the context.**

**Analyze functions using different representations.**

## Building Functions

**Build a function that models a relationship between two quantities.**

# Geometry

## Expressing Geometric Properties with Equations

**Translate between the geometric description and the equation for a conic section.**

# Statistics and Probability

## Interpreting Categorical and Quantitative Data

**Summarize, represent, and interpret data on a single count or measurement variable.**

## Making Inferences and Justifying Conclusions

**Understand and evaluate random processes underlying statistical experiments.**

**Make inferences and justify conclusions from sample surveys, experiments, and observational studies.**

# Conditional Probability and the Rules of Probability

**Understand independence and conditional probability and use them to interpret data.**

**Use the rules of probability to compute probabilities of compound events in a uniform probability model.**

# Using Probability to Make Decisions

**Use probability to evaluate outcomes of decisions.**

Some of the assessment items for the Standards for Mathematical Content cited in the preceding Contents also involve one or more of the following Standards for Mathematical Practice.

# Standards for Mathematical Practice

| | |
|---|---|
| **MP.1** | Make sense of problems and persevere in solving them. |
| **MP.2** | Reason abstractly and quantitatively. |
| **MP.3** | Construct viable arguments and critique the reasoning of others. |
| **MP.4** | Model with mathematics. |
| **MP.5** | Use appropriate tools strategically. |
| **MP.6** | Attend to precision. |
| **MP.7** | Look for and make use of structure. |
| **MP.8** | Look for and express regularity in repeated reasoning. |

# N.RN.1 Answers

1. B

2. A

3. D

4. B, C, F

5. A

6. B

7. G

8. D

9. $\left(b^{\frac{1}{4}}\right)^4 = b^{\frac{1}{4} \cdot 4} = b$, so $b^{\frac{1}{4}}$ is the fourth root of $b$ by definition. Thus, it makes sense that $\sqrt[4]{b} = b^{\frac{1}{4}}$.

**Rubric**

3 points for a logically sound explanation

10.
$$\sqrt[3n]{a^{2m}} = \sqrt[3(4m)]{a^{2m}}$$
$$= \sqrt[12m]{a^{2m}}$$
$$= a^{\frac{2m}{12m}}$$
$$= a^{\frac{1}{6}}$$

**Rubric**

1 point for rewriting $\sqrt[3n]{a^{2m}}$ as $\sqrt[12m]{a^{2m}}$;

1 point for rewriting $\sqrt[12m]{a^{2m}}$ as $a^{\frac{2m}{12m}}$;

1 point for rewriting $a^{\frac{2m}{12m}}$ as $a^{\frac{1}{6}}$ (Score similarly if students choose to substitute $\frac{1}{4}n$ for $m$ and then rewrite and simplify.)

11. $\left(x^{\frac{4}{3}}\right)^3 = x^{\frac{4}{3} \cdot 3} = x^4$, which means that $x^{\frac{4}{3}}$ is the cube root of $x^4$ by definition. Thus, it makes sense that $\sqrt[3]{x^4} = x^{\frac{4}{3}}$.

**Rubric**

3 points for a logically sound explanation

12. a. Use any negative number for $x$, for example:

$$\sqrt[4]{x^2} \overset{?}{=} \sqrt{x}$$
$$\sqrt[4]{(-9)^2} \overset{?}{=} \sqrt{-9}$$
$$\sqrt[4]{81} \overset{?}{=} \sqrt{-9}$$
$$3 \neq \sqrt{-9}$$

b. The statement is true only for nonnegative values of $x$.

**Rubric**

a. 1 point for giving an example of a number that makes the statement true; 1 point for showing why the given value doesn't work

b. 2 points for a correct restriction

1. B

2. D

3. A

4. A, E

5.

$$\left(c^{-9}d^{12}\right)^{-\frac{5}{6}} = \left(c^{-9}\right)^{-\frac{5}{6}}\left(d^{12}\right)^{-\frac{5}{6}}$$

$$= c^{-9\left(-\frac{5}{6}\right)}d^{12\left(-\frac{5}{6}\right)}$$

$$= c^{\frac{15}{2}} \cdot d^{-10}$$

$$= \frac{c^{\frac{15}{2}}}{d^{10}}$$

**Rubric**

1 point for the correct answer; 2 points for showing appropriate work

6. $\dfrac{1}{t^{-\frac{2}{5}}}$, $\left(\sqrt[3]{t^2}\right)^{\frac{4}{7}}$, $\sqrt[6]{t} \cdot \sqrt[8]{t}$, $\dfrac{t}{t^{\frac{5}{7}}}$

**Rubric**

2 points for the correct answer

7. The expression $\left[\left(d^{\frac{1}{3}}\right)^{\frac{1}{7}}\right]^{\frac{1}{4}}$ has a real

number result when $d \geq 0$.

If $d$ is negative, then $d^{\frac{1}{3}}$ is also negative.

If $d^{\frac{1}{3}}$ is negative, then $\left(d^{\frac{1}{3}}\right)^{\frac{1}{7}}$ is also

negative. Raising a quantity to $\dfrac{1}{4}$ is the

same as taking the fourth root, and there is no real fourth root of a negative number.

**Rubric**

1 point for the correct answer; 2 points for a logically sound explanation

8.

$$\left(a^{-\frac{1}{m}}\right)^{-\frac{1}{n}} = a^{-\frac{1}{m}\left(-\frac{1}{n}\right)} = a^{\frac{1}{mn}} = \sqrt[mn]{a}$$

$$\left[\left(jk^4\right)^{-\frac{1}{5}}\right]^{-\frac{1}{3}} = 5 \cdot \sqrt[3]{jk^4} = \sqrt[15]{jk^4}$$

**Rubric**

2 points for showing $\left(a^{-\frac{1}{m}}\right)^{-\frac{1}{n}} = \sqrt[mn]{a}$;

2 points for showing $\left[\left(jk^4\right)^{-\frac{1}{5}}\right]^{-\frac{1}{3}} = \sqrt[15]{jk^4}$

9. a. In the first step, Terrell divided the exponents when he should have subtracted them.

b.

$$\frac{x^{\frac{1}{3}}}{x^{\frac{2}{5}}} = x^{\frac{1}{3} - \frac{2}{5}} = x^{-\frac{1}{15}} = \frac{1}{\sqrt[15]{x}}$$

c. They are equivalent; in the expression

$\dfrac{x^{\frac{1}{3}}}{x^{\frac{2}{5}}}$, a negative value of $x$ means the

numerator will be negative and the denominator will be positive (because it is the equivalent of taking the 5th root of the square of a negative number, which is always positive), giving a negative result. In the

expression $\dfrac{1}{\sqrt[15]{x}}$, a negative value of $x$

simplifies to 1 over a negative number, which also gives a negative result.

**Rubric**

a. 1 point for identifying the error

b. 1 point for answer; 1 point for adequate work

c. 1 point for answer; 2 points for appropriate explanation

# N.Q.2* Answers

1. A

2. C

3. A, C

4. a. The independent variable is the time $t$, in hours, after 6 a.m. The dependent variable is $c$, the number of cars on the highway at time $t$.

   b. The vertex of the parabola occurs when $t = 2$ (because 8 a.m. is 2 hours after 6 a.m.) and $c = 6500$. So, the function has form $c(t) = a(t - 2)^2 + 6500$. To find the value of $a$, substitute 0 for $t$ and 4000 for $c(t)$ to get $4000 = a(0 - 2)^2 + 6500$, so $a = \dfrac{-2500}{4} = -625$. Therefore, $c(t) = -625(t - 2)^2 + 6500$.

## Rubric

   a. 1 point for appropriate variable names; 1 point for identifying the independent and dependent variables

   b. 2 points for correct reasoning; 1 point for function

5. a. The volume depends on the side length of the square cut from each corner of the cardboard. Let $s$ be the length of one side of the square.

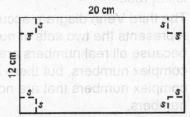

   b. The length of the box will be the length of the cardboard (20 cm) minus the side lengths of the two squares cut from the corners ($2s$). So, an expression to represent the length of the box is $20 - 2s$. Similarly, the width of the box will be the width of the cardboard minus the side lengths of the two squares, or $12 - 2s$.

The height of the box will be the side length of the squares cut from each corner. When the flaps are folded up, they form the sides of the box, which are each $s$ cm tall.

   c. $V = \ell w h$
   $$= (20 - 2s)(12 - 2s)s$$
   $$= 4s^3 - 64s^2 + 240s$$

## Rubric

   a. 1 point for description of variable and assigning a letter; 1 point for labeling the diagram

   b. 1 point for explaining each dimension

   c. 1 point

6. a. Let $a$ represent the age of the child, in years. Let $h_c$ represent the height of the chair seat, measured in inches. Let $h_t$ represent the height of the table, measured in inches.

   b. In a model relating the height of the chair seat to the age of the child, $a$ is the independent variable and $h_c$ is the dependent variable, since the age of the child determines the appropriate height of the chair. Similarly, in a model relating the height of the table to the age of the child, $a$ is the independent variable and $h_t$ is the dependent variable, since the age of the child determines the appropriate height of the table.

   c. For heights given as ranges, find the mean of the least and greatest values of the range. The mean serves as a "typical" or representative height for that range.

## Rubric

   a. 1 point for each variable description

   b. 1 point for each model

   c. 1 point

# N.CN.1 Answers

1. C

2. C

3. C, D

4. C

5. F

6. B

7. G

8. H

9. The equation has two real solutions, ±2, and two non-real solutions, ±2$i$.

   **Rubric**

   1 point for each solution

10. a. $\sqrt{144} - \sqrt{64} = 12 - 8 = 4$; this result is a real number.

    b. $\sqrt{144} + \sqrt{-64} = 12 + 8i$; this result is a non-real number.

    **Rubric**

    For each part: 1 point for simplifying; 1 point for identifying the type of number

11. The equation has no real solutions and two non-real solutions: $i\sqrt{5}$ and $-i\sqrt{5}$. Since the equation has no real solutions, the graph has no $x$-intercepts.

    **Rubric**

    1 point for identifying no real solutions; 1 point for identifying the two non-real solutions; 1 point for describing the graph

12. The statement is imprecise because while the equation has no solution in the set of real numbers, it does have two solutions in the set of complex numbers.

$$25x^2 + 27 = 0$$
$$25x^2 = -27$$
$$x^2 = -\frac{27}{25}$$
$$x = \pm\sqrt{-\frac{27}{25}}$$
$$x = \pm\frac{3i\sqrt{3}}{5}$$

**Rubric**

1 point for explanation; 1 point for each solution

13. a. Yes, every real number is also a complex number. By definition, a complex number has the form $a + bi$ where $a$ and $b$ are real numbers and $i = \sqrt{-1}$. If you let $b = 0$, then the complex number $a + 0i$, or simply $a$, is just a real number.

    b. No, every complex number is not also a real number. For instance, the complex number $0 + bi$, or simply $bi$, is not real.

    c. The third Venn diagram accurately represents the two sets of numbers because all real numbers are also complex numbers, but there are complex numbers that are not real numbers.

    **Rubric**

    a. 1 point for saying yes; 1 point for explanation

    b. 1 point for saying no; 1 point for explanation

    c. 1 point for choosing the third Venn diagram; 1 point for the explanation

# N.CN.2 Answers

1. C
2. B
3. B, C, F
4. G
5. A
6. D
7. F
8. H
9. C

10. $a + b = (1 - 4i) + (3 + 3i) = 4 - i$
    $a - b = (1 - 4i) - (3 + 3i) = -2 - 7i$
    $ab = (1 - 4i)(3 + 3i) = 15 - 9i$

**Rubric**

1 point each for answer

11.

| | |
|---|---|
| $i(a + bi) = ia + i(bi)$ | Distributive prop. |
| $= ai + (bi)i$ | Commutative prop. of mult. |
| $= ai + bi^2$ | Associative prop. of mult. and definition of squaring |
| $= ai + b(-1)$ | $i^2 = -1$ |
| $= b(-1) + ai$ | Commutative prop. of add. |
| $= -b + ai$ | Mult. prop. of $-1$ |

**Rubric**

1 point for each missing property

12. $(a + bi)(3 - 6i) = 3a - 6ai + 3bi + 6b$
    For this expression to be a real number, the imaginary terms $-6ai$ and $3bi$ must have a sum of 0, which means that $-6a + 3b = 0$ or $b = 2a$. One possible pair of values is $a = 1$ and $b = 2$. For those values of $a$ and $b$,
    $(a + bi)(3 - 6i) = (1 + 2i)(3 - 6i)$
    $= 3 - 12i^2$
    $= 3 - (-12)$
    $= 15$

**Rubric**

1 point each for acceptable values of $a$ and $b$; 1 point for correct simplification

13. a. $(3 + 4i)(3 + 4i) = -7 + 24i$
    b. $(3 + 4i)(3 - 4i) = 25$
    c. $(a + bi)(a + bi) = (a^2 - b^2) + 2abi$
       $(a + bi)(a - bi) = a^2 + b^2$

**Rubric**

a. 1 point
b. 1 point
c. 1 point for each identity

14.

| | |
|---|---|
| $i$ | $\sqrt{-1}$ |
| $i^2$ | $-1$ |
| $i^3$ | $-\sqrt{-1}$ |
| $i^4$ | $1$ |
| $i^5$ | $\sqrt{-1}$ |
| $i^6$ | $-1$ |
| $i^7$ | $-\sqrt{-1}$ |
| $i^8$ | $1$ |

If the remainder of $n \div 4$ is 1, $i^n = \sqrt{-1}$.

If the remainder is 2, $i^n = -1$.

If the remainder is 3, $i^n = -\sqrt{-1}$.

If the remainder is 0, $i^n = 1$.

- $i^9 = \sqrt{-1}$ because $9 \div 4$ has a remainder of 1.
- $i^{26} = -1$ because $26 \div 4$ has a remainder of 2.
- $i^{100} = 1$ because $100 \div 4$ has a remainder of 0.

**Rubric**

1 point for completing the table; 1 point for describing the pattern; 1 point for each answer

# N.CN.7 Answers

1. B

2. B

3. C, F

4. B

5. A

6. F

7. C

8. The equation has two non-real solutions.

$$x = -\frac{3}{4} \pm \frac{\sqrt{3}}{4}i$$

**Rubric**
1 point for solution description;
1 point for each solution

9. a. $5x^2 + 3x + 1 = 0$

   b. The equation has two non-real solutions.

   c. $x = -\frac{3}{10} \pm \frac{\sqrt{11}}{10}i$

**Rubric**
a. 1 point
b. 1 point
c. 1 point for each solution

10. Marco is not correct. When solving for $x$ using the quadratic formula, Marco likely made the discriminant positive.

Marco's possible work:

$$x = \frac{-6 \pm \sqrt{36 - 52}}{2}$$

$$= \frac{-6 \pm \sqrt{16}}{2}$$

$$= -3 \pm 2$$

$$= -1, -5$$

Correct work:

$$x = \frac{-6 \pm \sqrt{36 - 52}}{2}$$

$$= \frac{-6 \pm \sqrt{-16}}{2}$$

$$= \frac{-6 \pm 4i}{2}$$

$$= -3 \pm 2i$$

**Rubric**
1 point for knowing that Marco is incorrect; 1 point for identifying and explaining the error; 1 point for each correct solution

11. a. The equation $4x^2 + 8x + c = 0$ has two non-real solutions when $c > 4$. The discriminant for the given quadratic equation, $b^2 - 4ac = 8^2 - 4(4)c$, must be less than 0 for the equation to have two non-real solutions.

$$8^2 - 4(4)c < 0$$
$$64 - 16c < 0$$
$$-16c < -64$$
$$c > 4$$

   b. $x = -1 \pm \frac{3}{2}i$

**Rubric**
a. 1 point for description of $c$;
   1 point for explanation
b. 1 point for each solution

12. The equations have the same number of solutions, but not the same type of solutions.

The first equation has two non-real solutions. The second equation has two real solutions.

The solutions of the first equation are $x = 2 \pm i\sqrt{17}$. The solutions of the second equation are $x = 3$ and $x = -7$.

**Rubric**
1 point for comparison; 1 point for the description of each equation's solutions; 1 point for the solutions of each equation

# N.CN.8(+) Answers

1. C
2. D
3. B
4. F
5. B
6. D

7. $(2x + 3i)(2x + 3i) = 0$; $x = -\dfrac{3}{2}i$

**Rubric**
1 point for factoring;
1 point for the solution

8. Method 1:
Factor the left side completely. Set each binomial equal to 0, and then solve for x.

Method 2:
Use properties of equality and the definition of a square root to isolate x on one side of the equation.

Solution 1:
$$9x^2 + 144 = 0$$
$$9(x^2 + 16) = 0$$
$$9(x + 4i)(x - 4i) = 0$$
$$x + 4i = 0 \quad \text{or} \quad x - 4i = 0$$
$$x = -4i \qquad\qquad x = 4i$$

Solution 2:
$$9x^2 + 144 = 0$$
$$9x^2 = -144$$
$$x^2 = -\dfrac{144}{9}$$
$$x^2 = -16$$
$$x = \pm\sqrt{-16}$$
$$x = \pm 4i$$

Both methods produce the same solutions.

**Rubric**
1 point for describing each method;
1 point for each correct solution process;
1 point for obtaining the same solutions

9.
$$x = \frac{-2 \pm \sqrt{(2)^2 - 4(1)(5)}}{2(1)} = \frac{-2 \pm \sqrt{-16}}{2} = \frac{-2 \pm 4i}{2} = -1 \pm 2i$$

So,
$$x^2 + 2x + 5 = [x - (-1 + 2i)][x - (-1 - 2i)].$$

**Rubric**
1 point for the solutions;
1 point for the factorization

10. a. $(2x + 7)^2 = 4x^2 + 28x + 49$
   $(2x + 7i)^2 = 4x^2 + 28ix - 49$

   b. The expanded forms of the two expressions have the same $x^2$-term. The x-terms differ in that the expanded form of $(2x + 7i)^2$ has a factor of i. The constants are opposites due to a factor of $i^2 = -1$ in the expanded form of $(2x + 7i)^2$.

   c. Both the $x^2$-term and the constant in the expansion of $(2ix + 7)^2$ will be the opposite of the corresponding term in the expansion of $(2x + 7i)^2$, but the x-terms in the two expansions will be the same.

**Rubric**
a. 1 point for each trinomial
b. 2 points for a correct comparison
c. 2 points for a correct description

11. $a^2 + b^2 = (a + bi)(a - bi)$
   This identity is similar to the difference-of-squares identity $a^2 - b^2 = (a + b)(a - b)$. However, in the new identity, the second term of each binomial is non-real, so the expression $a^2 + b^2$ is factored as the product of two non-real numbers.

   $$144x^2 + 25y^2 = (12x + 5iy)(12x - 5iy)$$
   $$144x^2 - 25y^2 = (12x + 5y)(12x - 5y)$$

**Rubric**
1 point for correct identity;
1 point for comparison to $a^2 - b^2$;
1 point for each factorization

# N.CN.9(+) Answers

1. D

2. A

3. A, C, E, F

4. a. 2

   b. 3

   c. 4

   d. 3

5. Since the polynomial has degree 2, it has 2 complex roots.

   $$x^2 + 4x + 12 = 0$$

   $$x = \frac{-4 \pm \sqrt{(4)^2 - 4(1)(12)}}{2(1)}$$

   $$x = -2 \pm 2i\sqrt{2}$$

   **Rubric**

   1 point for correct number of complex roots; 1 point for each root

6. Sheila is incorrect. The quadratic polynomial $x^2 - 18x + 81$ has the factored form $(x - 9)^2$. This means the real root 9 is a repeated root. The polynomial has two complex roots, but both are 9.

   **Rubric**

   1 point for stating that Sheila is incorrect; 1 point for explanation; 1 point for stating the second complex root

7. a. The left side of the equation is the product of three polynomials, each with degree 2. By the corollary of the fundamental theorem of algebra, the number of complex roots for each of these polynomials is 2. So, the total number of complex solutions is $2 + 2 + 2 = 6$.

   b. $x = 2i, -2i, 2, -2, -3, -3$

   **Rubric**

   a. 1 point for correct answer; 1 point for reasoning

   b. 0.5 point for each solution

8. a. By the corollary of the fundamental theorem of algebra, the degree of a polynomial equals the number of complex roots provided repeated roots are counted multiple times. So, a polynomial with two complex roots (neither of which is repeated) must have degree 2.

   b. Multiplying the polynomial from part a by any nonzero constant will produce another polynomial with degree 2. The complex roots of the new polynomial are the same as the original roots, since multiplying by a constant does not change the roots.

   c. Multiplying the polynomial by the binomial $x - c$ produces a polynomial with the original roots and one more, $c$.

   **Rubric**

   a. 1 point

   b. 1 point for description; 1 point for roots

   c. 1 point for description; 1 point for root

9. The solutions of a quadratic equation written in the form $ax^2 + bx + c = 0$, where $a$, $b$, and $c$ are real numbers (with $a \neq 0$), are $x = \dfrac{-b \pm \sqrt{b^2 - 4ac}}{2a}$. This form has three possible cases.

   1. 1 repeated real solution when $b^2 - 4ac = 0$

   2. 2 real solutions when $b^2 - 4ac > 0$

   3. 2 non-real solutions when $b^2 - 4ac < 0$

   In all cases, the quadratic equation has 2 solutions, which matches the degree of the polynomial $ax^2 + bx + c$. So, the quadratic formula supports the corollary of the fundamental theorem of algebra, which says that a polynomial of degree $n$ has $n$ complex roots provided repeated roots are counted multiple times.

   **Rubric**

   1 point for stating the quadratic formula; 1 point for analysis of each of the three solution cases; 1 point for conclusion

# A.SSE.1.a* Answers

1. C

2. B

3. F

4. D

5. A

6. E

7. The expression $x + 2$ represents the length of each side of the square region A.

   The expression $(x + 2)^2$ represents the area of region A.

   The expression $(2x + 5)(3x - 2)$ represents the area of the entire rectangular mat.

   **Rubric**

   1 point for each description

8. a. The first term, $2\pi r^2$, represents the combined area of the two circles used as the bases of the cylinder. The second term, $2\pi rh$, represents the area of the rectangle that is rolled into a circle to create the lateral surface of the cylinder.

   b. No. In the first term, the 2 is used to indicate that there are 2 identical circles used as the bases of the cylinder. The 2 in the second term indicates that the width of the rectangle is $2\pi r$, the circumference of each circular base.

   c. $2\pi r^2 + 2\pi rh = 2\pi(3)^2 + 2\pi(3)(6) =$

   $18\pi + 36\pi = 54\pi \approx 169.65$

   The surface area of Andre's cylinder is about 170 square inches.

   **Rubric**

   a. 1 point for the interpretation of each term

   b. 1 point for correct answer; 1 point for explanation

   c. 1 point

9. a. This represents her starting salary.

   b. This represents the factor by which her annual salary is multiplied at the end of each year.

   c. This represents the factor by which her starting salary is multiplied after she has worked for $n$ years.

   **Rubric**

   1 point for each description

10. Dividing $x^3 + 3x^2 - 6x - 8$ by $x - 2$ gives $x^2 + 5x + 4$. This expression represents the area of the base of the box.

    **Rubric**

    1 point for correct polynomial expression; 1 point for interpretation

11. If you let $t$ represent the number of days it would take Janine to build the set working alone, then the fraction for Janine is $\dfrac{5}{t}$, and the fraction for Adam is $\dfrac{6}{t+3}$.

    In the expression $\dfrac{5}{t}$, 5 represents the number of days that Janine has worked, and $t$ represents the number of days for Janine to build the set working alone. In the expression $\dfrac{6}{t+3}$, 6 represents the number of days that Adam has worked, and $t + 3$ represents the number of days for Adam to build the set working alone.

    **Rubric**

    1 point for each expression; 1 point for each interpretation

# A.SSE.1b* Answers

1. B

2. D

3. C

4. D

5. The expression $s^2$ represents the area of the vase's square base. The expression $4sh$ represents the combined area of the vase's 4 rectangular sides.

   **Rubric**
   1 point for each correct interpretation

6. a. The term $12\pi r^3$ corresponds to the combined volume of the spheres.

   b. The term $5s^3$ corresponds to the combined volume of the cubes.

   c. The term $\pi r^2 s$ corresponds to the combined volume of the cones.

   d. The volume of a sphere with radius $r$ is $\frac{4}{3}\pi r^3$. Because $12\pi r^3 = 9 \cdot \frac{4}{3}\pi r^3$, there are 9 spheres.

   e. The volume of a cube with side length $s$ is $s^3$. Because $5s^3 = 5 \cdot s^3$, there are 5 cubes.

   f. The volume of a cone with radius $r$ and height $s$ is $\frac{1}{3}\pi r^2 s$. Because $\pi r^2 s = 3 \cdot \frac{1}{3}\pi r^2 s$, there are 3 cones.

   **Rubric**
   1 point for each part

7. The expressions $\frac{A}{h}$ and $45 - h - \frac{A}{h}$ represent the width and length, respectively, of the carry-on luggage.

   **Rubric**
   1 point for each correct interpretation

8. The area of a circle is $\pi r^2$, so the expression $2\pi r^2$ is the sum of the areas of the top and bottom of the cylindrical can. The volume of a cylinder with height $h$ is $V = \pi r^2 h$, so $\frac{V}{r} = \pi r h$ and $\frac{2V}{r} = 2\pi r h$.

Since $2\pi r$ is the circumference of a base of the cylindrical can, $2\pi r h$ is the area of the curved surface connecting the two bases. So, $\frac{2V}{r}$ represents the lateral surface area.

**Rubric**
1 point for each correct interpretation;
1 point for each explanation

9. a. In the expression, the term $\frac{d}{10}$ represents the time in seconds that Karl runs on the beach because it is the quotient of a distance $d$, in feet, and Karl's running rate of 10 feet per second. The term $\frac{\sqrt{30^2 + (72-d)^2}}{3}$ represents the time in seconds that Karl swims. The distance Karl swims is $\sqrt{30^2 + (72-d)^2}$, which is the hypotenuse of a right triangle with legs of length 30 feet and $(72 - d)$ feet, as shown below. Dividing this distance by Karl's swimming rate of 3 feet per second gives the swimming time.

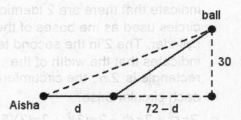

b. The distance from Aisha to the ball is the hypotenuse of a right triangle with legs of length 72 feet and 30 feet.
   $$\sqrt{72^2 + 30^2} = 78$$
   So, Aisha threw the ball 78 feet.

**Rubric**
a. 2 points for interpreting each term
b. 2 points

# A.SSE.2* Answers

1. B

2. C

3. D, E

4. F

5. C

6. A

7. D

8. $x^6 - 729$

$$= \left(x^3\right)^2 - 27^2$$

$$= \left(x^3 + 27\right)\left(x^3 - 27\right)$$

$$= \left(x^3 + 3^3\right)\left(x^3 - 3^3\right)$$

$$= (x + 3)\left(x^2 - 3x + 9\right)(x - 3)\left(x^2 + 3x + 9\right)$$

**Rubric**

2 points for accurate work; 1 point for correct answer

9.

$$p_0 \cdot 1.07^{t+10} = p_0 \cdot 1.07^t \cdot 1.07^{10}$$

$$\approx p_0 \cdot 1.07^t \cdot 1.967$$

Since $p_0 \cdot 1.07^t$ is the present value of the investment, the value 10 years later will be almost double the present value.

**Rubric**

1 point for rewriting the expression;
1 point for conclusion

10. Instead of writing $a^6 - b^6$ as the difference of two cubes, Bill should start by writing $a^6 - b^6$ as the difference of two squares.

$$a^6 - b^6$$

$$= \left(a^3\right)^2 - \left(b^3\right)^2$$

$$= \left(a^3 + b^3\right)\left(a^3 - b^3\right)$$

$$= (a + b)\left(a^2 - ab + b^2\right)(a - b)\left(a^2 + ab + b^2\right)$$

While it is relatively easy to see that multiplying $a^2 - ab + b^2$ and $a^2 + ab + b^2$ gives $a^4 + a^2b^2 + b^4$, it is difficult to see that $a^4 + a^2b^2 + b^4$ factors as $\left(a^2 - ab + b^2\right)\left(a^2 + ab + b^2\right)$.

**Rubric**

2 points for starting over and using the difference of two squares; 1 point for the complete factorization

11. The total amount of money Justin raises for running $m$ miles is $250 + 40m$, so the total amount of money he raises per mile is $\dfrac{250 + 40m}{m}$.

$$\frac{250 + 40m}{m} = \frac{250}{m} + \frac{40m}{m}$$

$$= \frac{250}{m} + 40$$

**Rubric**

2 points for each expression

12. a. The profit Luize makes is the difference between her sales and her costs. Her sales are \$3.50 per print, and her costs are \$2 per print as well as a fixed \$30. So, the expression for Luize's profit from selling $p$ prints is $3.5p - 2p - 30 = 1.5p - 30$.

  b. Luize's profit per print is the quotient of her total profit and the number of prints she sells. Her total profit is $1.5p - 30$, so her profit per print is $\dfrac{1.5p - 30}{p}$.

  c.

  $$\frac{1.5p - 30}{p} = \frac{1.5p}{p} - \frac{30}{p}$$

  $$= 1.5 - \frac{30}{p}$$

  d. Luize's profit per print increases. As the value of $p$ increases in the expression $1.5 - \dfrac{30}{p}$, the value of $\dfrac{30}{p}$ decreases. So, Luize's profit per print will get closer and closer to \$1.50.

**Rubric**

a. 1 point

b. 1 point

c. 2 points

d. 1 point for answer; 1 point for explanation

# A.SSE.3c* Answers

1. C

2. B

3. A

4. B, D

5.

$$81^{\frac{7}{5}x} = \left(3^4\right)^{\frac{7}{5}x}$$

$$= 3^{\frac{28}{5}x}$$

$$= \left(27^{\frac{1}{3}}\right)^{\frac{28}{5}x}$$

$$= 27^{\frac{28}{15}x}$$

**Rubric**

1 point for work; 1 point for answer

6. a. $f(t) = 64\left(\dfrac{1}{2}\right)^{\frac{t}{3}}$

b. Since $t$ is measured in days, $t$ has to be divided by 7 to measure weeks. In order to change the exponent from $\dfrac{t}{3}$ to $\dfrac{t}{7}$, multiply it by $\dfrac{3}{7}$. Compensate for introducing a factor of $\dfrac{3}{7}$ by also introducing a factor of $\dfrac{7}{3}$ because $\dfrac{3}{7} \cdot \dfrac{7}{3} = 1$.

$$f(t) = 64\left(\frac{1}{2}\right)^{\frac{7}{3} \cdot \frac{3}{7} \cdot \frac{t}{3}}$$

$$= 64\left(\left(\frac{1}{2}\right)^{\frac{7}{3}}\right)^{\frac{t}{7}}$$

$$\approx 64(0.1984)^{\frac{t}{7}}$$

So, the percent remaining after one week is about 20%.

**Rubric**

a. 1 point for recognizing the value of $a$; 1 point for recognizing the value of $c$

b. 2 points for reasoning; 1 point for writing an equivalent function; 1 point for the percent remaining after each week

7.

$$g(x) = 4^{\frac{3}{2}x}$$

$$= 4^{\frac{1}{2}x + x}$$

$$= 4^{\frac{1}{2}x} \cdot 4^x$$

$$= \left(4^{\frac{1}{2}}\right)^x \cdot 4^x$$

$$= 2^x \cdot 4^x$$

$$= 2^x \cdot f(x)$$

So, the value of $g(x)$ is $2^x$ times greater than the value of $f(x)$ for any value of $x$.

**Rubric**

2 points for rewriting $g(x)$; 1 point for answer

8. a. Because $t$ is measured in years, the quarterly interest rate can be found by rewriting the exponent as $4t$. Compensate for introducing a factor of 4 by also introducing a factor of $\dfrac{1}{4}$ because $\dfrac{1}{4} \cdot 4 = 1$.

$$4600(1.05)^t = 4600(1.05)^{\frac{1}{4} \cdot 4 \cdot t}$$

$$= 4600\left((1.05)^{\frac{1}{4}}\right)^{4t}$$

$$\approx 4600(1.012)^{4t}$$

So, the approximate quarterly interest rate is 1.2%.

12

b. Because *t* is measured in years, the monthly interest rate can be found by rewriting the exponent as 12*t*. Compensate for introducing a factor of 12 by also introducing a factor of $\frac{1}{12}$ because $\frac{1}{12} \cdot 12 = 1$.

$$4600(1.05)^t = 4600(1.05)^{\frac{1}{12} \cdot 12 \cdot t}$$

$$= 4600\left((1.05)^{\frac{1}{12}}\right)^{12t}$$

$$\approx 4600(1.004)^{12t}$$

So, the approximate monthly interest rate is 0.4%.

c. To rewrite $4600(1.012)^{4t}$ so that the exponent is 12*t*, introduce a factor of 3 in the exponent, and compensate by also introducing a factor of $\frac{1}{3}$.

$$4600(1.012)^{4t} = 4600(1.012)^{\frac{1}{3} \cdot 3 \cdot 4t}$$

$$= 4600\left(1.012^{\frac{1}{3}}\right)^{12t}$$

$$\approx 4600(1.004)^{12t}$$

The only drawback to this method is that the base 1.012 is a rounded decimal, so rounding again when finding the value of $1.012^{\frac{1}{3}}$ could lead to an inaccurate result.

d. The annual interest rate, 5%, is the fourth power of the quarterly interest rate, 1.2%, and the quarterly interest rate is the third power of the monthly interest rate, 0.4%. (Equivalently, the monthly interest rate is the cube root of the quarterly interest rate, and the quarterly interest rate is the fourth root of the annual interest rate.)

**Rubric**

a. 1 point for explaining reasoning and showing work; 1 point for the quarterly interest rate

b. 1 point for explaining reasoning and showing work; 1 point for the monthly interest rate

c. 1 point for describing the method; 1 point for showing that the method works; 1 point for stating drawback

d. 1 point for stating the relationship among the interest rates

9. Because *t* is measured in decades, the annual growth rate can be found by rewriting the exponent as 10*t*. Compensate for introducing a factor of 10 by also introducing a factor of $\frac{1}{10}$ because $\frac{1}{10} \cdot 10 = 1$.

$$P(t) = 18,800(1.58)^t$$

$$= 18,800(1.58)^{\frac{1}{10} \cdot 10 \cdot t}$$

$$= 18,800\left((1.58)^{\frac{1}{10}}\right)^{10t}$$

$$\approx 18,800(1.047)^{10t}$$

The population of Dallas, Texas, was growing at a rate of about 58% per decade from 1880 to 1970. This is equivalent to an annual growth rate of about 4.7%.

**Rubric**

1 point for explaining reasoning; 1 point for showing work; 1 point for identifying the growth rate by decade; 1 point for identifying the growth rate by year

# A.SSE.4* Answers

1. B

2. C

3. A, E

4. a. No
   b. Yes
   c. Yes
   d. No
   e. No

5. Find the difference $S_n - rS_n$:

$$S_n - rS_n = a + ar + ar^2 + ar^3 + \ldots + ar^{n-1} -$$
$$(ar + ar^2 + ar^3 + \ldots + ar^{n-1} + ar^n)$$
$$= a - ar^n$$

Then factor $S_n - rS_n$ and $a - ar^n$ to get
$(1 - r)S_n = a(1 - r^n)$.

Finally, divide both sides of the equation

by $1 - r$ to get $S_n = a\left(\dfrac{1 - r^n}{1 - r}\right)$.

6. Use the formula for the sum of a finite geometric series with $a = 200$, $r = 1.05$, and $n = 4$.

$$200\left(\frac{1 - 1.05^4}{1 - 1.05}\right) = 862.025$$

The account balance is \$862.03 at the time that the fourth deposit is made.

**Rubric**

1 point for accurate work; 1 point for correct answer

7. Since the ball bounces up and down, the total vertical distance for any given bounce is twice the height of the bounce. The sequence of bounce heights is therefore 40, 40(0.75), $40(0.75)^2$, ... . The total vertical distance traveled by the ball after $n$ bounces is the sum of the series $40 + 40(0.75) + 40(0.75)^2 + \ldots + 40(0.75)^{n-1}$, or $S_n = 40\left(\dfrac{1 - 0.75^n}{1 - 0.75}\right)$.

When $n = 10$, the sum is

$$S_{10} = 40\left(\frac{1 - 0.75^{10}}{1 - 0.75}\right) \approx 151. \text{ So, after}$$

10 bounces, the ball has traveled about 151 feet vertically.

**Rubric**

1 point for correct reasoning that leads to the general formula; 1 point for writing the general formula; 1 point for evaluating the formula for $n = 10$

8. Use the formula for the sum of a finite geometric series with $a = 32$, $r = 0.5$, and $n = 6$. Note that $a \neq 36$ and $n \neq 7$ because the first round is not a part of the geometric series.

$$\text{Games played} = 4 + S_6$$
$$= 4 + 32\left(\frac{1 - 0.5^6}{1 - 0.5}\right)$$
$$= 4 + 63$$
$$= 67$$

A total of 67 games were played.

**Rubric**

0.5 point for correctly identifying the value of $a$; 0.5 point for correctly identifying the value of $n$; 1 point for accurate work, including correct use of formula; 1 point for correct answer

9. a. The monthly interest rate is $0.06 \div 12 = 0.005$. The value of the untouched debt after 7 years, or 84 months, would be $25,000(1.005)^{84} \approx 38,009.24$. If Shauna did nothing to pay off her debt, its value would be about \$38,009.24 in 7 years.

   b. Because $38,009.24 \div 84 \approx 452.49$, the monthly payment needed to pay \$38,009.24 in equal amounts over 7 years is about \$452.49.

c. Shauna will not actually be paying a total of $38,009.24. Provided the monthly payments are large enough to cover the monthly interest and reduce the principal, the principal will decrease from month to month and therefore accrue less interest each month.

d. Let $p$ be the monthly payment.

After 1 month, the balance will be $B = 25{,}000(1.005) - p$.

After 2 months, the balance will be $B = [25{,}000(1.005) - p](1.005) - p$, which can be rewritten as $B = 25{,}000(1.005)^2 - p(1.005) - p$.

After 3 months, after being rewritten, the balance will be
$B = 25{,}000(1.005)^3 - (1.005)^2 - p(1.005) - p$.

Extend the pattern: After $n$ months, the balance will be
$B = 25{,}000(1.005)^n - p(1.005)^{n-1} - p(1.005)^{n-2} - \ldots - p(1.005) - p$.

You can factor $p$ out of all of the terms except for the first, so rewrite the balance as
$B = 25{,}000(1.005)^n - p\left(1.005^{n-1} + 1.005^{n-2} + \ldots + 1.005 + 1\right)$.

The expression inside the parentheses is a geometric series with $n$ terms and a common ratio $r = 1.005$, so use the formula for the sum of a finite geometric series to rewrite the balance as shown below.

$$B = 25{,}000(1.005)^n - p\left(\frac{1-1.005^n}{1-1.005}\right)$$

$$= 25{,}000(1.005)^n - p\left(\frac{1.005^n - 1}{0.005}\right)$$

The debt will be paid off when $B = 0$, so substitute 0 for $B$ and 84 for $n$ and then solve for $p$.

$$0 = 25{,}000(1.005)^{84} - p\left(\frac{1.005^{84} - 1}{0.005}\right)$$

$$p\left(\frac{1.005^{84} - 1}{0.005}\right) = 25{,}000(1.005)^{84}$$

$$p = \frac{25{,}000(1.005)^{84}}{\dfrac{1.005^{84} - 1}{0.005}}$$

$$p = \frac{0.005(25{,}000)(1.005^{84})}{1.005^{84} - 1}$$

$$p \approx 365.21$$

So, Shauna's minimum monthly payment is $365.21.

**Rubric**

a. 1 point

b. 1 point

c. 1 point

d. 3 points for accurate work; 1 point for correct answer

# A.APR.1 Answers

1. D

2. A

3. C

4. B, C, E

5. $(3x-2)(2x^2-5x+1) = 6x^3 - 15x^2 + 3x - 4x^2 + 10x - 2$
$$= 6x^3 - 19x^2 + 13x - 2$$

**Rubric**

1 point for work; 1 point for correct product

6. $(5x^4 - x^3 + 2x + 1) + (2x^3 + 3x^2 - 4x - 7) = 5x^4 + 2x^3 - x^3 + 3x^2 + 2x - 4x + 1 - 7$
$$= 5x^4 + x^3 + 3x^2 - 2x - 6$$

**Rubric**

1 point for work; 1 point for correct sum

7. a.
$$M_A(t) - M_B(t) = -0.006t^4 - 0.025t^3 + 1.25t^2 + 2.5t + 31 -$$
$$(-0.003t^4 - 0.15t^3 + 2.25t^2 + 1.25t + 19)$$
$$= -0.006t^4 - 0.025t^3 + 1.25t^2 + 2.5t + 31 +$$
$$0.003t^4 + 0.15t^3 - 2.25t^2 - 1.25t - 19$$
$$= -0.003t^4 + 0.125t^3 - t^2 + 1.25t + 12$$

b. The polynomial $M_A(t) - M_B(t)$ represents how many more students were members of club A than club B.

**Rubric**

a. 1 point for correct difference; 1 point for correct work

b. 1 point for reasonable description

8. a. The volume of rectangular prism A is $V_A = x^3 + 8x^2 + 17x + 10$.
The volume of rectangular prism B is $V_B = x^3 + 8x^2 + 21x + 18$.

b. The polynomials for $V_A$ and $V_B$ have the same $x^3$-terms and the same $x^2$-terms. While the coefficients of the $x$-terms and the constants are positive for both polynomials, the polynomial for $V_B$ has a greater $x$-term coefficient and a greater constant. So, $V_B > V_A$ for $x \geq 0$.

c. The positive difference in the volumes is $V_B - V_A = 4x + 8$.

**Rubric**

a. 1 point for a correct expression for the volume of prism A;
1 point for a correct expression for the volume of prism B

b. 1 point for identifying the prism with the greater volume;
1 point for explanation

c. 1 point for a correct expression for the difference

9. a.

| Set | Closed under addition? | Closed under subtraction? | Closed under multiplication? | Closed under division? |
|---|---|---|---|---|
| Whole numbers | Yes | No | Yes | No |
| Integers | Yes | Yes | Yes | No |
| Rational numbers | Yes | Yes | Yes | Yes |
| Real numbers | Yes | Yes | Yes | Yes |

b. Example showing that the set of whole numbers is not closed under subtraction: $1 - 2 = -1$, which is not a whole number. Example showing that the set of whole numbers is not closed under division: $1 \div 2 = 0.5$, which is not a whole number. Example showing that the set of integers is not closed under division: $-1 \div 2 = -0.5$, which is not an integer.

c. The set of polynomials is closed under addition, subtraction, and multiplication. It is not closed under division. For instance, $(2x - 1) \div x = 2 - \dfrac{1}{x}$, which is not a polynomial.

d. With respect to closure, the set of polynomials is most like the set of integers.

**Rubric**

1 point for each part

# A.APR.2 Answers

1. D

2. B

3. B

4. A, D, F

5. a. No

  b. Yes

  c. Yes

  d. No

  e. Yes

6.

$$p(4) = 4^4 - 4(4)^3 - 11(4)^2 + 66(4) - 72$$
$$= 256 - 256 - 176 + 264 - 72$$
$$= 16$$

So, the remainder is 16.

$$
\require{enclose}
\begin{array}{r}
x^3 \phantom{xxxxx} -11x + 22 \\
x-4 \enclose{longdiv}{x^4 - 4x^3 - 11x^2 + 66x - 72} \\
\end{array}
$$

$$-\left(x^4 - 4x^3\right)$$
$$0 - 11x^2 + 66x$$
$$-\left(-11x^2 + 44x\right)$$
$$22x - 72$$
$$-(22x - 88)$$
$$16$$

**Rubric**

1 point for correct application of remainder theorem; 1 point for correct remainder; 1 point for correct long division

7. Use synthetic substitution to find $p(5)$:

```
5| 1  -7    2   40
       5  -10  -40
   1  -2   -8    0
```

The last number in the bottom row of the synthetic substitution array is $p(5)$. Since $p(5) = 0$, $x - 5$ is a factor of $p(x)$. The coefficients of the quotient when $p(x)$ is divided by $x - 5$ are the first three numbers in the bottom row of the synthetic substitution array. So, $p(x) = (x - 5)(x^2 - 2x - 8)$.

Factoring the quadratic factor by inspection gives $(x + 2)(x - 4)$, so the complete factorization of $p(x)$ is $p(x) = (x - 5)(x + 2)(x - 4)$.

**Rubric**

1 point for showing $x - 5$ is a factor of $p(x) = x^3 - 7x^2 + 2x + 40$;

1 point for finding $x + 2$ as a factor;

1 point for finding $x - 4$ as a factor

8. a. The factor theorem says that for a polynomial $p(x)$ and a number $a$, $p(a) = 0$ if and only if $x - a$ is a factor of $p(x)$. Tyrell's calculations were correct for $a = 4$, but he then said that $x + a$ was a factor of the polynomial instead of $x - a$.

  b. From Tyrell's work, $x - 4$ is a factor of $p(x)$. Divide $p(x)$ by $x - 4$ to obtain a quadratic factor.

$$
\require{enclose}
\begin{array}{r}
x^2 - 5x + 6 \\
x-4 \enclose{longdiv}{x^3 - 9x^2 + 26x - 24} \\
\end{array}
$$

$$-\left(x^3 - 4x^2\right)$$
$$-5x^2 + 26x$$
$$-\left(-5x^2 + 20x\right)$$
$$6x - 24$$
$$-(6x - 24)$$
$$0$$

The quadratic factor $x^2 - 5x + 6$ can be factored as $(x - 3)(x - 2)$, so the three linear factors of $p(x)$ are $x - 4$, $x - 3$, and $x - 2$.

**Rubric**

a. 1 point for correctly identifying the mistake; 1 point for a reasonable explanation

b. 1 point for each factor

9. a. There appears to be a zero at $x = 6$.

$$p(6) = 6^3 - 9(6)^2 + 24(6) - 36$$
$$= 216 - 324 + 144 - 36$$
$$= 0$$

This result confirms that the function has a zero at $x = 6$.

b. Divide $p(x)$ by $x - 6$.

$$
\begin{array}{r}
x^2 - 3x + 6 \\
x - 6 \overline{) x^3 - 9x^2 + 24x - 36} \\
\underline{-(x^3 - 6x^2)} \\
-3x^2 + 24x \\
\underline{-(-3x^2 + 18x)} \\
6x - 36 \\
\underline{-(6x - 36)} \\
0
\end{array}
$$

So, $p(x) = (x - 6)(x^2 - 3x + 6)$.

c. Evaluate the factor $x^2 - 3x + 6$ to see whether $x = 6$ is a repeated zero.

$6^2 - 3(6) + 6 = 24$

Since the value of $x^2 - 3x + 6$ for $x = 6$ is not 0, 6 is not a repeated zero.

d. The graph of $p(x)$ does not cross the $x$-axis anywhere other than at $x = 6$, so by the remainder theorem, there are no other real values of $a$ such that the division of $p(x)$ by $x - a$ results in a remainder of 0. And, by the factor theorem, there are no other real values of $a$ such that $x - a$ is a factor of $p(x)$.

**Rubric**

a. 1 point for identifying the zero; 1 point for showing it is a zero

b. 1 point

c. 1 point

d. 2 points

# A.APR.3 Answers

1. D

2. C

3. A, B, F

4. a. Yes

   b. No

   c. Yes

   d. No

   e. No

5. a. $p(x) = -x(x - 3)(x - 3)(x + 2)$;
   $x = 0$, $x = 3$, $x = 3$, $x = -2$

   b.

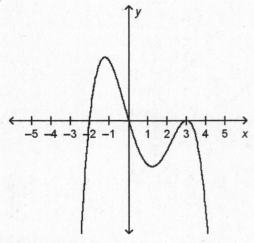

**Rubric**

a. 0.5 point for each zero

b. 0.5 point for showing the graph
   crossing the x-axis at $x = -2$;
   0.5 point for showing the graph
   crossing the x-axis at $x = 0$;
   0.5 point for showing the graph
   tangent to the x-axis at $x = 3$;
   0.5 for downward end behavior at both
   ends of the graph

6. a. $p(x) = (x - 2)(x - 2)(x + 2)$;
   $x = 2$, $x = 2$, $x = -2$

   b.

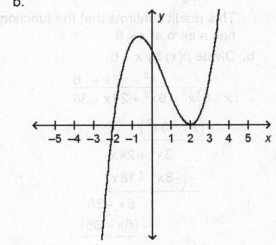

**Rubric**

a. 0.5 point for each zero

b. 0.5 point for showing the graph
   crossing the x-axis at $x = -2$;
   1 point for showing the graph tangent
   to the x-axis at $x = 2$;
   0.5 for showing downward end
   behavior at the left end;
   0.5 point for showing upward end
   behavior at the right end

7. If you are given a complete list of zeros of
   an unknown polynomial function, you
   know that the graph must intersect the
   x-axis at those zeros. Moreover, the
   number of times any given zero occurs
   tells you whether the graph crosses the
   x-axis or is tangent to the x-axis at that
   zero. But this information alone does not
   tell you whether the graph lies above or
   below the x-axis in between the zeros, or
   what the end behavior of the graph is.

   Although the zeros determine the variable
   factors in the function's rule, you do not
   know whether the rule includes a
   constant factor as well. The sign of the
   constant factor would tell you the graph's
   end behavior, and from that you can
   deduce whether the graph lies above or
   below the x-axis in between the zeros.

## Rubric

1 point for recognizing that a complete list of zeros is insufficient for sketching a graph; 1 point for explaining why the graph cannot be sketched; 1 point for identifying what additional information is needed

8. a. If $D(t)$ has any integer zeros, they must be factors of 28: $\pm 1, \pm 2, \pm 4, \pm 7, \pm 14, \pm 28$. If 1 is a zero, then $t - 1$ would be a factor of $D(t)$. Try dividing $t^3 - 12t^2 + 39t - 28$ by $t - 1$:

$$
\begin{array}{r}
t^2 - 11t + 28 \\
t - 1 \overline{)\, t^3 - 12t^2 + 39t - 28} \\
-\left(t^3 - \ t^2\right) \\
\hline
-11t^2 + 39t \\
-\left(-11t^2 + 11t\right) \\
\hline
28t - 28 \\
-\left(28t - 28\right) \\
\hline
0
\end{array}
$$

So, you can write the function as follows:

$$D(t) = -\frac{1}{12}(t - 1)\left(t^2 - 11t + 28\right)$$

$$= -\frac{1}{12}(t - 1)(t - 4)(t - 7)$$

The zeros of the function are 1, 4, and 7, so the telethon is at the target average at the end of the first, fourth, and seventh hours.

b.

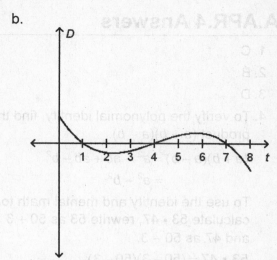

c. A factor of $t - 10$ would have to be introduced into the model so that the graph of the function would cross the $t$-axis at $t = 10$. Also, the constant factor would need to be positive to produce the desired end behavior (rising above the $t$-axis for $t > 10$). (Extra: To make the new model produce values that roughly match the values of the original model, the constant factor would need to be changed from $-\frac{1}{12}$ to $\frac{1}{120}$.)

## Rubric

a. 0.5 point each for identifying the first, fourth, and seventh hours

b. 0.5 point each for showing the graph crossing the $t$-axis at $t = 1$, $t = 4$, and $t = 7$;
0.5 point for showing upward end behavior at the left end of the graph;
0.5 point for showing downward end behavior at the right end of the graph

c. 1 point for recognizing that a factor of $t - 10$ would need to be introduced;
1 point for recognizing that the constant factor must become positive

# A.APR.4 Answers

1. C

2. B

3. D

4. To verify the polynomial identity, find the product $(a + b)(a - b)$.

$$(a+b)(a-b) = a^2 - ab + ab - b^2$$
$$= a^2 - b^2$$

To use the identity and mental math to calculate $53 \cdot 47$, rewrite 53 as $50 + 3$ and 47 as $50 - 3$.

$$53 \cdot 47 = (50+3)(50-3)$$
$$= 50^2 - 3^2$$
$$= 2500 - 9$$
$$= 2491$$

**Rubric**

1 point for correctly simplifying the product $(a + b)(a - b)$; 1 point for substituting correct values of $a$ and $b$; 1 point for using the identity to calculate the product

5. To verify the polynomial identity, find the product $(a + b)(a + b)(a + b)$.

$$(a+b)^3 = (a+b)(a+b)(a+b)$$
$$= \left(a^2 + 2ab + b^2\right)(a+b)$$
$$= a^3 + a^2b + 2a^2b + 2ab^2 + ab^2 + b^3$$
$$= a^3 + 3a^2b + 3ab^2 + b^3$$

Comparing $(3x + 2)^3$ to $(a + b)^3$ shows that $3x$ corresponds to $a$ and 2 corresponds to $b$. Substitute $3x$ for $a$ and 2 for $b$ in the identity and simplify to write $(3x + 2)^3$ in expanded form.

$$(a+b)^3 = a^3 + 3a^2b + 3ab^2 + b^3$$
$$(3x+2)^3 = (3x)^3 + 3(3x)^2(2) + 3(3x)(2)^2 + 2^3$$
$$= 27x^3 + 3(9x^2)(2) + 3(3x)(4) + 8$$
$$= 27x^3 + 54x^2 + 36x + 8$$

**Rubric**

1 point for correctly simplifying the product $(a + b)^3$;
1 point for correct substitutions in the identity;
1 point for the correct expanded form

6.

$$(10a+b)^2 = (10a+b)(10a+b)$$
$$= 100a^2 + 20ab + b^2$$

The identity is
$(10a + b)^2 = 100a^2 + 20ab + b^2$.

Since $57 = 10 \cdot 5 + 7$, 5 corresponds to $a$ and 7 corresponds to $b$ in the identity.

$$(10a+b)^2 = 100a^2 + 20ab + b^2$$
$$(10 \cdot 5 + 7)^2 = 100(5)^2 + 20 \cdot 5 \cdot 7 + 7^2$$
$$= 2500 + 700 + 49$$
$$= 3249$$

So, $57^2 = 3249$.

**Rubric**

1 point for deriving the identity;
1 point for substituting correct values of $a$ and $b$ in the identity;
1 point for the correct answer

7. Write $31^3$ as $(30 + 1)^3$, so 30 corresponds to $a$ and 1 corresponds to $b$ in the identity.

$$(a+b)^3 = a^3 + 3a^2b + 3ab^2 + b^3$$
$$(30+1)^3 = 30^3 + 3(30)^2(1) + 3(30)(1)^2 + 1^3$$
$$= 27,000 + 3(900) + 3(30) + 1$$
$$= 27,000 + 2700 + 90 + 1$$
$$= 29,791$$

Write $29^3$ as $(30 - 1)^3$, so 30 corresponds to $a$ and 1 corresponds to $b$ in the identity.

$$(a-b)^3 = a^3 - 3a^2b + 3ab^2 - b^3$$
$$(30-1)^3 = 30^3 - 3(30)^2(1) + 3(30)(1)^2 - 1^3$$
$$= 27,000 - 3(900) + 3(30) - 1$$
$$= 27,000 - 2700 + 90 - 1$$
$$= 24,389$$

**Rubric**

1 point each for using each identity correctly; 1 point each for each correct value

8. a. In the expression $(a - b)^3$, $-b$ corresponds to $b$ in the identity for $(a + b)^3$. Substitute $-b$ for $b$ in the identity $(a + b)^3 = a^3 + 3a^2b + 3ab^2 + b^3$ and simplify.

$$(a + b)^3 = a^3 + 3a^2b + 3ab^2 + b^3$$
$$(a + (-b))^3 = a^3 + 3a^2(-b) + 3a(-b)^2 + (-b)^3$$
$$= a^3 - 3a^2b + 3ab^2 - b^3$$

b.

$$(a + b)^3 - (a - b)^3 = (a^3 + 3a^2b + 3ab^2 + b^3) -$$
$$(a^3 - 3a^2b + 3ab^2 - b^3)$$
$$= a^3 + 3a^2b + 3ab^2 + b^3 -$$
$$a^3 + 3a^2b - 3ab^2 + b^3$$
$$= 6a^2b + 2b^3$$
$$= 2b(3a^2 + b^2)$$

(Note that $6a^2b + 2b^3$, $2(3a^2b + b^3)$, and $2b(3a^2 + b^2)$ are all acceptable answers.)

c. Note that $42 = 40 + 2$ and $38 = 40 - 2$. Substitute 40 for $a$ and 2 for $b$ in the identity and simplify.

$$(a + b)^3 - (a - b)^3 = 6a^2b + 2b^3$$
$$(40 + 2)^3 - (40 - 2)^3 = 6(40)^2(2) + 2(2)^3$$
$$= 6(1600)(2) + 2(8)$$
$$= 19,200 + 16$$
$$= 19,216$$

The difference in the volumes of the two containers is 19,216 cm$^3$.

**Rubric**
a. 1 point
b. 1 point
c. 1 point for substituting correct values of $a$ and $b$; 1 point for correct answer

9. a.

$$(2m)^2 + (m^2 - 1)^2 = 4m^2 + m^4 - 2m^2 + 1$$
$$= m^4 + 2m^2 + 1$$
$$= (m^2 + 1)^2$$

b. The table shows some values of $m$ and the corresponding Pythagorean triples where $a = 2m$, $b = m^2 - 1$, and $c = m^2 + 1$.

| $m$ | $a$ | $b$ | $c$ | Primitive? |
|---|---|---|---|---|
| 2 | 4 | 3 | 5 | Yes |
| 3 | 6 | 8 | 10 | No |
| 4 | 8 | 15 | 17 | Yes |
| 5 | 10 | 24 | 26 | No |

It appears that the identity generates primitive Pythagorean triples only when $m$ is even.

c. When $m$ is odd, $2m$ is even, $m^2 - 1$ is even, and $m^2 + 1$ is even. If all the numbers in a Pythagorean triple are even, then they have 2 as a common factor, so the Pythagorean triple is not primitive.

**Rubric**
1 point for each part

Algebra 2 Teacher Guide       **23**       Common Core Assessment Readiness

# A.APR.5(+) Answers

1. D
2. C
3. C
4. A
5. B
6. D
7. F
8. E
9. C

10. Comparing the expressions $(a - b)^5$ and $(a + b)^n$ shows that $a$ corresponds to $a$, $-b$ corresponds to $b$, and 5 corresponds to $n$ in the binomial theorem. The fifth row of Pascal's triangle gives $_5C_0 = 1$, $_5C_1 = 5$, $_5C_2 = 10$, $_5C_3 = 10$, $_5C_4 = 5$, and $_5C_5 = 1$.

$$(a+b)^n = {_nC_0}a^n b^0 + {_nC_1}a^{n-1}b^1 + {_nC_2}a^{n-2}b^2 + \cdots + {_nC_{n-1}}a^1 b^{n-1} + {_nC_n}a^0 b^n$$

$$(a-b)^5 = 1a^5(-b)^0 + 5a^4(-b)^1 + 10a^3(-b)^2 + 10a^2(-b)^3 + 5a^1(-b)^4 + 1a^0(-b)^5$$

$$= a^5 - 5a^4 b + 10a^3 b^2 - 10a^2 b^3 + 5ab^4 - b^5$$

The polynomial identity is $(a-b)^5 = a^5 - 5a^4 b + 10a^3 b^2 - 10a^2 b^3 + 5ab^4 - b^5$.

**Rubric**

1 point for substituting correctly for $a$, $b$, and $n$ in the binomial theorem;
1 point for substituting the correct values from Pascal's triangle;
1 point for simplifying correctly

11. Comparing the expressions $(x - 2y)^7$ and $(a + b)^n$ shows that $x$ corresponds to $a$, $-2y$ corresponds to $b$, and 7 corresponds to $n$ in the binomial theorem. The $x^5 y^2$-term of the simplified expanded form is the third term produced by the binomial theorem. Use Pascal's triangle to determine that $_7C_2 = 21$.

$$_7C_2 a^5 b^2 = 21(x)^5(-2y)^2$$

$$= 84x^5 y^2$$

The $x^5 y^2$-term in the expanded form of $(x - 2y)^7$ is $84x^5 y^2$.

**Rubric**

1 point for identifying the correct term of the binomial theorem to use;
1 point for substituting correctly for $a$, $b$, and $n$ in the binomial theorem;
1 point for simplifying correctly

12. Comparing the expressions $(3x^2 + 2)^3$ and $(a + b)^n$ shows that $3x^2$ corresponds to $a$, 2 corresponds to $b$, and 3 corresponds to $n$ in the binomial theorem. The third row of Pascal's triangle gives $_3C_0 = 1$, $_3C_1 = 3$, $_3C_2 = 3$, and $_3C_3 = 1$.

$$(a+b)^n = {_nC_0}a^n b^0 + {_nC_1}a^{n-1}b^1 + {_nC_2}a^{n-2}b^2 + \cdots + {_nC_{n-1}}a^1 b^{n-1} + {_nC_n}a^0 b^n$$

$$(3x^2 + 2)^2 = 1(3x^2)^3(2)^0 + 3(3x^2)^2(2)^1 + 3(3x^2)^1(2)^2 + 1(3x^2)^0(2)^3$$

$$= (3x^2)^3 + 3(3x^2)^2(2) + 3(3x^2)(2)^2 + (2)^3$$

$$= 27x^6 + 6(9x^4) + 3(3x^2)(4) + 8$$

$$= 27x^6 + 54x^4 + 36x^2 + 8$$

**Rubric**

1 point for substituting correctly for $a$, $b$, and $n$ in the binomial theorem;
1 point for substituting the correct values from Pascal's triangle;
1 point for simplifying correctly

13. Shifting the graph of $f(x)$ 1 unit to the left means that $g(x) = f(x + 1)$. So, replace $x$ with $x + 1$ in $f(x) = 2x^3 - x^2 + 3x - 4$.

$$f(x) = 2x^3 - x^2 + 3x - 4$$

$$g(x) = f(x+1) = 2(x+1)^3 - (x+1)^2 + 3(x+1) - 4$$

Use the binomial theorem to expand $(x + 1)^3$. Comparing the expressions $(x + 1)^3$ and $(a + b)^n$ shows that $x$ corresponds to $a$, 1 corresponds to $b$, and 3 corresponds to $n$ in the binomial theorem. The third row of Pascal's triangle gives $_3C_0 = 1$, $_3C_1 = 3$, $_3C_2 = 3$, and $_3C_3 = 1$.

$$(a+b)^3 = 1a^3 b^0 + 3a^2 b^1 + 3a^1 b^2 + 1a^0 b^3$$

$$(x+1)^3 = 1x^3 1^0 + 3x^2 1^1 + 3x^1 1^2 + 1x^0 1^3$$

$$= x^3 + 3x^2 + 3x + 1$$

Now replace the powers of $x + 1$ in the rule for $g(x)$ with their expanded forms and simplify.

$$g(x) = 2(x+1)^3 - (x+1)^2 + 3(x+1) - 4$$

$$= 2(x^3 + 3x^2 + 3x + 1) - (x^2 + 2x + 1) + 3x + 3 - 4$$

$$= 2x^3 + 6x^2 + 6x + 2 - x^2 - 2x - 1 + 3x + 3 - 4$$

$$= 2x^3 + 5x^2 + 7x$$

**Rubric**

1 point for recognizing that $g(x) = f(x + 1)$;
1 point for using the binomial theorem to expand $(x + 1)^3$;
1 point for expanding $(x + 1)^2$ correctly (with or without using the binomial theorem);
1 point for simplifying the rule for $g(x)$

14. Use the binomial theorem to expand $(x^2 + (x - 1))^3$. Comparing the expressions $(x^2 + (x - 1))^3$ and $(a + b)^n$ shows that $x^2$ corresponds to $a$, $x - 1$ corresponds to $b$, and 3 corresponds to $n$ in the binomial theorem. The third row of Pascal's triangle gives ${}_3C_0 = 1$, ${}_3C_1 = 3$, ${}_3C_2 = 3$, and ${}_3C_3 = 1$.

$$(a + b)^n = {}_nC_0 a^n b^0 + {}_nC_1 a^{n-1} b^1 + {}_nC_2 a^{n-2} b^2 + \cdots + {}_nC_{n-1} a^1 b^{n-1} + {}_nC_n a^0 b^n$$

$$(a + b)^3 = a^3 + 3a^2 b + 3ab^2 + b^3$$

$$(x^2 + (x - 1))^3 = (x^2)^3 + 3(x^2)^2(x - 1) + 3(x^2)(x - 1)^2 + (x - 1)^3$$

Use $a = x$, $b = -1$, $n = 3$, and the third row of Pascal's triangle to expand $(x - 1)^3$.

$$(a + b)^3 = a^3 + 3a^2 b + 3ab^2 + b^3$$

$$(x - 1)^3 = x^3 + 3x^2(-1) + 3x(-1)^2 + (-1)^3$$

$$= x^3 - 3x^2 + 3x - 1$$

Now replace the powers of $x - 1$ in the expansion of $(x^2 + (x - 1))^3$ with their expanded forms and simplify.

$$(x^2 + (x - 1))^3 = (x^2)^3 + 3(x^2)^2(x - 1) + 3(x^2)(x - 1)^2 + (x - 1)^3$$

$$= x^6 + 3x^4(x - 1) + 3x^2(x^2 - 2x + 1) + (x^3 - 3x^2 + 3x - 1)$$

$$= x^6 + 3x^5 - 3x^4 + 3x^4 - 6x^3 + 3x^2 + x^3 - 3x^2 + 3x - 1$$

$$= x^6 + 3x^5 - 5x^3 + 3x - 1$$

Note: The same result can be obtained by expanding $((x^2 + x) - 1)^3$ or $((x^2 - 1) + x)^3$.

**Rubric**

2 points for correctly using the binomial theorem to expand $(x^2 + (x - 1))^3$ as a product of monomials and powers of $x - 1$;

1 point for expanding $(x - 1)^3$ correctly;

1 point for expanding $(x - 1)^2$ correctly;

1 point for expressing the polynomial in standard form

# A.APR.6 Answers

1. D

2. B

3. A, C, D, E

4.

$$3x^2 + x + 2$$
$$2x^2+5x+3\overline{)6x^4+17x^3+18x^2+13x+6}$$
$$\underline{-(6x^4+15x^3+9x^2)}$$
$$2x^3+9x^2+13x$$
$$\underline{-(2x^3+5x^2+3x)}$$
$$4x^2+10x+6$$
$$\underline{-(4x^2+10x+6)}$$
$$0$$

Since the remainder is 0, the quotient has no rational term and is just the polynomial $3x^2 + x + 2$.

**Rubric**

1 point for dividing correctly; 1 point for explaining that the quotient is just a polynomial

5. The height is the volume divided by the product of the length and width,
$$\frac{x^3+10x^2+31x+30}{(x+5)(x+2)}.$$

Multiply in the denominator to get
$$\frac{x^3+10x^2+31x+30}{(x+5)(x+2)} =$$
$$\frac{x^3+10x^2+31x+30}{x^2+7x+10}, \text{ and then divide.}$$

$$x+3$$
$$x^2+7x+10\overline{)x^3+10x^2+31x+30}$$
$$\underline{-(x^3+7x^2+10x)}$$
$$3x^2+21x+30$$
$$\underline{-(3x^2+21x+30)}$$
$$0$$

The height of the rectangular prism is $x + 3$ centimeters.

**Rubric**

1 point for dividing to determine the height; 1 point for the correct height

6.

$$x^2+2x-3$$
$$x^2+4\overline{)x^4+2x^3+x^2+8x-9}$$
$$\underline{-(x^4+4x^2)}$$
$$2x^3-3x^2+8x$$
$$\underline{-(2x^3+8x)}$$
$$-3x^2-9$$
$$\underline{-(-3x^2-12)}$$
$$3$$

$$\frac{x^4+2x^3+x^2+8x-9}{x^2+4} = x^2+2x-3+\frac{3}{x^2+4}$$

**Rubric**

1 point for dividing correctly;
1 point for rewriting the expression in the correct form

7. a. Factor out $\frac{4}{3}\pi$ from the terms of the expression for the volume of the sphere to determine an expression for $r^3$.

$$\frac{256}{3}\pi x^3 - 192\pi x^2 + 144\pi x - 36\pi =$$
$$\frac{4}{3}\pi\left(64x^3 - 144x^2 + 108x - 27\right)$$

So, $r^3 = 64x^3 - 144x^2 + 108x - 27$.

b. Factor out $\pi$ from the terms of the expression for the area of the circle to determine an expression for $r^2$.

$$16\pi x^2 - 24\pi x + 9\pi = \pi(16x^2 - 24x + 9)$$

So, $r^2 = 16x^2 - 24x + 9$.

c.

$$\frac{r^3}{r^2} = \frac{64x^3 - 144x^2 + 108x - 27}{16x^2 - 24x + 9}$$

$$= \frac{64x^3 - 96x^2 - 48x^2 + 36x + 72x - 27}{16x^2 - 24x + 9}$$

$$= \frac{4x(16x^2 - 24x + 9) - 3(16x^2 - 24x + 9)}{16x^2 - 24x + 9}$$

$$= 4x - 3$$

The radius of the sphere is $4x - 3$ feet.

**Rubric**

a. 1 point for a correct expression for $r^3$

b. 1 point for a correct expression for $r^2$

c. 1 point for dividing correctly; 1 point for a correct expression for $r$

8. First, find the quotient $\dfrac{2x^2 + 11x - 23}{x + 7}$.

$$\begin{array}{r}
2x - 3 \\
x + 7 \overline{)\,2x^2 + 11x - 23} \\
-(2x^2 + 14x) \\
\hline
-3x - 23 \\
-(-3x - 21) \\
\hline
-2
\end{array}$$

$$\frac{2x^2 + 11x - 23}{x + 7} = 2x - 3 - \frac{2}{x + 7}$$

Now, compare $2x - 3 - \dfrac{2}{x + 7}$ to

$2x + a - \dfrac{2}{x + 7}$. The value of $a$ is $-3$.

**Rubric**

1 point for dividing correctly;
1 point for the correct value of $a$

9.

$$\begin{array}{r}
x - 4 \\
x^2 + 3x - 2 \overline{)\,x^3\ -\ x^2\ +\ ax\ +\ b} \\
-(x^3 + 3x^2\ -\ 2x) \\
\hline
-4x^2 + (a + 2)x + b \\
-(-4x^2\ -\ 12x + 8) \\
\hline
(a + 14)x + b - 8
\end{array}$$

$$\frac{x^3 - x^2 + ax + b}{x^2 + 3x - 2} = x - 4 + \frac{(a + 14)x + b - 8}{x^2 + 3x - 2}$$

So, $a + 14 = 2$ and $b - 8 = 1$.

$$a + 14 = 2 \qquad b - 8 = 1$$
$$a = -12 \qquad b = 9$$

**Rubric**

2 points for dividing correctly;
1 point for the value of $a$;
1 point for the value of $b$

# A.APR.7(+) Answers

1. D

2. A, C

3. a. Yes
   b. Yes
   c. Yes
   d. Yes
   e. Yes

4. $\dfrac{x^2+x-6}{x^2-6x-7} \div \dfrac{x^2-9x+14}{x^2+4x+3}$

$= \dfrac{(x-2)(x+3)}{(x-7)(x+1)} \div \dfrac{(x-2)(x-7)}{(x+3)(x+1)}$

$= \dfrac{(x-2)(x+3)}{(x-7)(x+1)} \cdot \dfrac{(x+3)(x+1)}{(x-2)(x-7)}$

$= \dfrac{(x-2)(x+3)^2(x+1)}{(x-7)^2(x+1)(x-2)}$

$= \dfrac{(x+3)^2}{(x-7)^2}$

$= \dfrac{x^2+6x+9}{x^2-14x+49}$

Excluded values: $x \neq -3, -1, 2, 7$

**Rubric**
1 point for correctly simplified expression; 1 point for accurate work; 0.25 point for each excluded value of $x$

5. $\dfrac{x^2-19}{x^2-x-56} - \dfrac{3}{x-8}$

$= \dfrac{x^2-19}{(x+7)(x-8)} - \dfrac{3(x+7)}{(x-8)(x+7)}$

$= \dfrac{x^2-19-3x-21}{(x+7)(x-8)}$

$= \dfrac{(x+5)(x-8)}{(x+7)(x-8)}$

$= \dfrac{x+5}{x+7}$

Excluded values: $x \neq -7, 8$

**Rubric**
1 point for correctly simplified expression; 1 point for accurate work; 0.5 point for each excluded value of $x$

6. Addition:

$\dfrac{p(x)}{q(x)} + \dfrac{r(x)}{s(x)} = \dfrac{p(x)s(x)}{q(x)s(x)} + \dfrac{q(x)r(x)}{q(x)s(x)}$

$= \dfrac{p(x)s(x)+q(x)r(x)}{q(x)s(x)}$

Since polynomials are closed under addition and multiplication, $p(x)s(x) + q(x)r(x)$ and $q(x)s(x)$ are polynomials, so $\dfrac{p(x)s(x)+q(x)r(x)}{q(x)s(x)}$ is a rational expression.

Subtraction:

$\dfrac{p(x)}{q(x)} - \dfrac{r(x)}{s(x)} = \dfrac{p(x)s(x)}{q(x)s(x)} - \dfrac{q(x)r(x)}{q(x)s(x)}$

$= \dfrac{p(x)s(x)-q(x)r(x)}{q(x)s(x)}$

Since polynomials are closed under subtraction and multiplication, $p(x)s(x) - q(x)r(x)$ and $q(x)s(x)$ are polynomials, so $\dfrac{p(x)s(x)-q(x)r(x)}{q(x)s(x)}$ is a rational expression.

Multiplication: $\dfrac{p(x)}{q(x)} \cdot \dfrac{r(x)}{s(x)} = \dfrac{p(x)r(x)}{q(x)s(x)}$

Since polynomials are closed under multiplication, $p(x)r(x)$ and $q(x)s(x)$ are polynomials, so $\dfrac{p(x)r(x)}{q(x)s(x)}$ is a rational expression.

Division:

$\dfrac{p(x)}{q(x)} \div \dfrac{r(x)}{s(x)} = \dfrac{p(x)}{q(x)} \cdot \dfrac{s(x)}{r(x)}$

$= \dfrac{p(x)s(x)}{q(x)r(x)}$

Since polynomials are closed under multiplication, $p(x)s(x)$ and $q(x)r(x)$ are polynomials, so $\dfrac{p(x)s(x)}{q(x)r(x)}$ is a rational expression.

**Rubric**
2 points for a reasonable justification for closure under each operation

7. a. Highway travel time $= \dfrac{50}{s}$,

town travel time $= \dfrac{10}{s-20}$

b. $\dfrac{50}{s} + \dfrac{10}{s-20} = \dfrac{50(s-20)}{s(s-20)} + \dfrac{10s}{s(s-20)}$

$= \dfrac{50s - 1000 + 10s}{s^2 - 20s}$

$= \dfrac{60s - 1000}{s^2 - 20s}$

c. $60 \div \dfrac{60s - 1000}{s^2 - 20s} = 60 \cdot \dfrac{s^2 - 20s}{60s - 1000}$

$= \dfrac{60s^2 - 1200s}{60s - 1000}$

$= \dfrac{20(3s^2 - 60s)}{20(3s - 50)}$

$= \dfrac{3s^2 - 60s}{3s - 50}$

**Rubric**

a. 0.5 point for each expression

b. 1 point for correct answer; 1 point for accurate work

c. 1 point for correct answer; 1 point for accurate work

8. a. When 0 is substituted for $x$ in

$\dfrac{x^2 + 8x - 33}{x^2 - 3x - 54} \div \dfrac{x^2 + 17x + 66}{x^2 - 12x + 27}$, the result

is $\dfrac{-33}{-54} \div \dfrac{66}{27} = \dfrac{33}{54} \cdot \dfrac{27}{66} =$

$\dfrac{33}{66} \cdot \dfrac{27}{54} = \dfrac{1}{2} \cdot \dfrac{1}{2} = \dfrac{1}{4}$, which is not the

result that Claire got.

b. Claire took the reciprocal of the first rational expression instead of the second rational expression when changing from division to multiplication.

c. $\dfrac{x^2 + 8x - 33}{x^2 - 3x - 54} \div \dfrac{x^2 + 17x + 66}{x^2 - 12x + 27}$

$= \dfrac{(x+11)(x-3)}{(x+6)(x-9)} \div \dfrac{(x+6)(x+11)}{(x-3)(x-9)}$

$= \dfrac{(x+11)(x-3)}{(x+6)(x-9)} \cdot \dfrac{(x-3)(x-9)}{(x+6)(x+11)}$

$= \dfrac{(x-3)^2}{(x+6)^2}$

**Rubric**

a. 1 point for a reasonable answer

b. 1 point for a reasonable answer

c. 1 point for a correctly simplified expression, 1 point for accurate work

# A.CED.1* Answers

1. B

2. C

3. D

4. A

5. A, D, E, H

6. Let $d$ represent the distance in miles from the lake to the fire. Use the fact that distance divided by rate equals time to write an inequality for the total time, which is 90 minutes, or 1.5 hours.

$$\frac{d}{294+14} + \frac{d}{294-14} \le 1.5$$

$$\frac{d}{308} + \frac{d}{280} \le 1.5$$

$$\frac{280d + 308d}{(308)(280)} \le 1.5$$

$$\frac{588d}{86,240} \le 1.5$$

$$588d \le 129,360$$

$$d \le 220$$

The fire is, at most, 220 miles from the lake.

**Rubric**

1 point for creating an appropriate inequality; 1 point for solving the inequality correctly; 1 point for answering the question

7. Let $t$ be the number of seconds after the red balloon begins to inflate. The volume of the red balloon is $1 \cdot 2^t$, and the volume of the blue balloon is $1 \cdot 4^{t-7}$ where $t \ge 7$. Solve the equation $2^t = 4^{t-7}$ for $t$.

$$2^t = 4^{t-7}$$

$$2^t = 2^{2(t-7)}$$

$$2^t = 2^{2t-14}$$

$$t = 2t - 14$$

$$14 = t$$

The volumes of the two balloons will be equal 14 seconds after the red balloon begins to inflate.

**Rubric**

1 point for creating an appropriate equation; 1 point for solving the equation correctly; 1 point for answering the question

8. Let $p$ be the average speed of the passenger train. The expression $\frac{420}{p}$ represents the time the passenger train needs to make the journey. The freight train averages 30 miles per hour slower than the passenger train, so the expression $\frac{420}{p-30}$ represents the time the freight train needs to make the journey, which is the greater time. The difference between the times for the freight train and the passenger train is $4\frac{1}{2}$ hours. Solve the equation $\frac{420}{p-30} - \frac{420}{p} = 4\frac{1}{2}$.

$$\frac{420}{p-30} - \frac{420}{p} = 4\frac{1}{2}$$

$$\frac{420p - 420(p-30)}{p(p-30)} = 4\frac{1}{2}$$

$$\frac{420p - 420p + 12,600}{p^2 - 30p} = 4\frac{1}{2}$$

$$\frac{12,600}{p^2 - 30p} = \frac{9}{2}$$

$$\frac{2}{9}(12,600) = p^2 - 30p$$

$$2800 = p^2 - 30p$$

$$0 = p^2 - 30p - 2800$$

$$0 = (p-70)(p+40)$$

Since the speed cannot be negative, the passenger train travels 70 miles per hour. This is the rate. Use the expression $\frac{420}{p}$ to calculate the time.

$$\frac{420}{70} = 6$$

The passenger train takes 6 hours to make the trip.

**Rubric**

1 point for creating an appropriate rate equation; 1 point for solving the equation for the rate; 1 point for the answer

9. The area of the rectangular enclosure is $(160 - 2x)x = 160x - 2x^2$. Solve the inequalities $160x - 2x^2 > 3000$ and $160x - 2x^2 < 3150$.

$$160x - 2x^2 > 3000$$
$$0 > 2x^2 - 160x + 3000$$
$$0 > x^2 - 80x + 1500$$
$$0 > (x - 30)(x - 50)$$

The right side of this inequality is negative when exactly one of the variable factors is negative. Both variable factors are negative for $x < 30$, the factor $x - 30$ is positive and the factor $x - 50$ is negative for $30 < x < 50$, and both variable factors are positive for $x > 50$. The area of the enclosure is greater than 3000 m$^2$ for 30 m $< x <$ 50 m.

$$160x - 2x^2 < 3150$$
$$0 < 2x^2 - 160x + 3150$$
$$0 < x^2 - 80x + 1575$$
$$0 < (x - 35)(x - 45)$$

The right side of this inequality is positive when both of the variable factors are negative or when both are positive. Both variable factors are negative for $x < 35$, the factor $x - 35$ is positive and the factor $x - 45$ is negative for $35 < x < 45$, and both variable factors are positive for $x > 45$. The area of the enclosure is less than 3150 m$^2$ for $x <$ 35 m or $x >$ 45 m.

The area of the enclosure is greater than 3000 m$^2$ for 30 m $< x <$ 50 m and less than 3150 m$^2$ for $x <$ 35 m or $x >$ 45 m.

So, for 30 m $< x <$ 35 m or 45 m $< x <$ 50 m, the area of the enclosure is greater than 3000 m$^2$ but less than 3150 m$^2$.

**Rubric**

2 points for appropriate inequalities; 2 points for solving the inequalities; 2 points for the correct ranges

10. If the boat and the ambulance arrive simultaneously, they travel for the same amount of time. Time is distance divided by rate. The time in hours for the ambulance to travel $70 - d$ miles at 75 miles per hour is $\dfrac{70 - d}{75}$. The boat travels $\sqrt{d^2 + 100}$ miles at 15 miles per hour, so the time in hours is $\dfrac{\sqrt{d^2 + 100}}{15}$.

Solve the equation $\dfrac{70 - d}{75} = \dfrac{\sqrt{d^2 + 100}}{15}$.

$$\frac{70 - d}{75} = \frac{\sqrt{d^2 + 100}}{15}$$
$$\frac{4900 - 140d + d^2}{5625} = \frac{d^2 + 100}{225}$$
$$4900 - 140d + d^2 = 5625\left(\frac{d^2 + 100}{225}\right)$$
$$d^2 - 140d + 4900 = 25(d^2 + 100)$$
$$d^2 - 140d + 4900 = 25d^2 + 2500$$
$$0 = 24d^2 + 140d - 2400$$
$$0 = 6d^2 + 35d - 600$$
$$0 = (3d + 40)(2d - 15)$$

Since the distance cannot be negative, $d = 7.5$. Point $C$ is 7.5 miles from point $B$.

**Rubric**

1 point for the travel time for the boat; 1 point for the travel time for the ambulance; 1 point for an appropriate equation; 1 point for solving for the value of $d$; 1 point for correct answer

# A.CED.2* Answers

1. B

2. A

3. $h = \dfrac{450}{\pi r^2}$

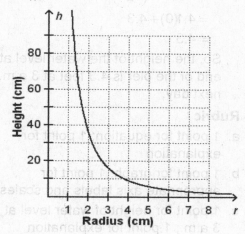

**Rubric**

1 point for equation; 1 point for curve; 1 point for appropriate axis labels and scales

4. $V = 20xy - 2x^2y - 2xy^2$

From the diagram, you can see that the length of each horizontal side of the rectangle is $2x + 2y$. Let $z$ be the length of each vertical side. Then the perimeter of the rectangle is $P = 2(2x + 2y) + 2z$.

Substituting 40 for $P$ and solving for $z$ gives $20 - 2x - 2y$. When the cardboard is folded, its open ends have dimensions $x$ feet by $y$ feet. The length of the box between the open ends is $20 - 2x - 2y$. So, the volume of the box is given by $V = xy(20 - 2x - 2y)$, or, equivalently, $V = 20xy - 2x^2y - 2xy^2$.

**Rubric**

1 point for equation; 2 points for explanation

5. a.  The general equation is $d = k\sqrt{h}$, where $k$ is a constant. Substitute 39 for $d$ and 1014 for $h$ in the equation.

$$39 = k\sqrt{1014}$$
$$39^2 = \left(k\sqrt{1014}\right)^2$$
$$1521 = 1014k^2$$
$$1.5 = k^2$$
$$1.22 \approx k$$

So, an equation is $d = 1.22\sqrt{h}$.

b.

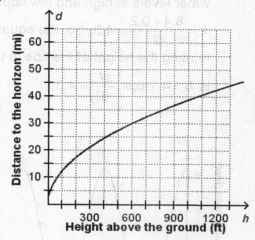

c.  No; because the equation involves taking the square root of $h$, the equation for the distance to the horizon is not linear. Doubling the height $h$ gives $2h$. Substituting $2h$ for $h$ in the equation gives the following.

$$d = 1.22\sqrt{2h}$$
$$= \sqrt{2}\left(1.22\sqrt{h}\right)$$

So, doubling the height multiplies the horizon distance by a factor of $\sqrt{2}$.

**Rubric**

a.  1 point for equation; 1 point for showing work

b.  1 point for curve; 1 point for appropriate axis labels and scales

c.  1 point for recognizing that doubling the height does not double the horizon distance; 1 point for recognizing the correct relationship of doubling height to horizon distance

---

6. a. You want an equation of the form

$h = a \cos\left(\dfrac{2\pi t}{b}\right) + k$. The period of the

tide is 12 hours, so $b = 12$. The amplitude $a$ is half of the difference between the high and low tides, so

$a = \dfrac{1}{2}(8.4 - 0.2) = 4.1$. Since $k$

determines the midline of the graph of the equation, $k$ is the average of the water levels at high and low tides, so

$k = \dfrac{8.4 + 0.2}{2} = 4.3$. So, the equation

relating the height of the tide to time

is $h = 4.1 \cos\left(\dfrac{\pi t}{6}\right) + 4.3$.

b.

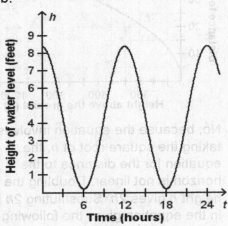

c. At 3 a.m. the next day, $t = 15$. Substitute 15 for $t$ in the equation.

$h = 4.1 \cos\left(\dfrac{15\pi}{6}\right) + 4.3$

$= 4.1 \cos\left(\dfrac{5\pi}{2}\right) + 4.3$

$= 4.1(0) + 4.3$

$= 4.3$

So, the height of the water level at the end of the pier is 4.3 feet at 3 a.m. the next day.

**Rubric**

a. 1 point for equation; 1 point for explanation

b. 1 point for graph; 1 point for appropriate axis labels and scales

c. 1 point for height of water level at 3 a.m.; 1 point for explanation

# A.CED.3* Answers

1. B

2. B

3. B, E

4. $0 < h < 18.5$;

   The volume function is described by $V(h) = h(45 - 2h)(37 - 2h)$. Since the length, width, and height of the box cannot be negative, the inequalities $h > 0$, $45 - 2h > 0$, and $37 - 2h > 0$ represent the constraints. Solving these inequalities, the constraints on $h$ are $h > 0$, $h < 22.5$, and $h < 18.5$. Since $18.5 < 22.5$, the shortest side of the box constrains the possible values of $h$. So, $0 < h < 18.5$.

   **Rubric**
   1 point for correct lower bound; 1 point for correct upper bound; 1 point for using $<$ signs instead of $\leq$ signs; 1 point for explanation

5. $c \geq 0$: Amber cannot produce a negative number of acres of corn.

   $w \geq 0$: Amber cannot produce a negative number of acres of wheat.

   $c + w \leq 200$: Amber cannot produce more than 200 combined acres of corn and wheat.

   $1.5c + w \leq 300$: Amber cannot spend more than 300 combined labor hours producing corn and wheat.

   **Rubric**
   0.5 point for each algebraic constraint; 0.5 point for each reasonable verbal explanation

6. a. No; since $c$ and $t$ represent numbers of calendars and T-shirts sold, they must have whole number values.

   b. Yes; for example, $(c, t) = (200, 40)$, $(100, 170)$, or any other ordered pair $(c, t)$ for which $0 < t < 300$ and $300 - t$ is a multiple of 13.

   c. No; in the real world, the art club would be happy to make *at least* $750, so the inequality $3.25c + 2.50t \geq 750$, which has many easily-found solutions with whole number coordinates, would make a better model.

   **Rubric**
   a. 1 point for answer and explanation
   b. 1 point for answer; 1 point for finding an example
   c. 1 point for answer and explanation

7. a. $r \geq 0$, $t \geq 0$, $\dfrac{1}{2}r + \dfrac{3}{4}t \leq 225$, $\dfrac{1}{2}r + \dfrac{1}{4}t \leq 150$

   b.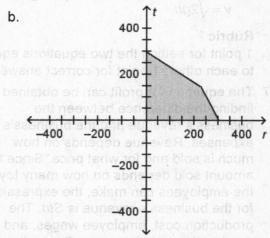

   c. The vertices of the shaded region are $(0, 0)$, $(0, 300)$, $(225, 150)$, and $(300, 0)$. Substituting each pair of $r$- and $t$-values in the profit function $P = 2.5r + 1.75t$ shows that the maximum value of $P$ occurs at $(225, 150)$, where $P = 825$. So, the maximum profit is $825 when 225 bottles of the regular juice blend and 150 bottles of the tropical juice blend are sold.

   **Rubric**
   a. 0.5 point for each constraint
   b. 0.5 point for accurate graph; 0.5 point for correctly shaded region
   c. 1 point for correct profit; 0.5 point for each correct number of bottles

# A.CED.4* Answers

1. D
2. C
3. A
4. B, C, E, G
5. A, D, E, G, H
6. Since the total amount of energy before the object falls is the same as when it hits the ground, the two formulas can be set equal to each other.

$$mgh = \frac{1}{2}mv^2$$

$$gh = \frac{1}{2}v^2$$

$$2gh = v^2$$

$$v = \sqrt{2gh}$$

**Rubric**

1 point for setting the two equations equal to each other; 1 point for correct answer

7. The equation for profit can be obtained by finding the difference between the business's revenue and the business's expenses. Revenue depends on how much is sold and for what price. Since the amount sold depends on how many toys the employees can make, the expression for the business's revenue is $Stn$. The production cost, employee wages, and overhead are all expenses. Production cost depends on the number produced and the cost per product, and it is found using the expression $Ctn$. Employee wages depend on the daily wage and the number of employees, and they are found using the expression $Wn$.

$$P = Stn - (Ctn + Wn + H)$$

$$P = Stn - Ctn - Wn - H$$

$$P + H = Stn - Ctn - Wn$$

$$P + H = n(St - Ct - W)$$

$$n = \frac{P + H}{St - Ct - W}$$

**Rubric**

2 points for explanation of how the profit equation is obtained;
1 point for correct profit equation;
1 point for solving profit equation for $n$

8. a. When $t = t_{0.5}$, half of the atoms of the isotope in the original sample have decayed. The number of atoms of the isotope remaining is $N = \frac{N_0}{2}$.

Substitute $t_{0.5}$ for $t$ and $\frac{N_0}{2}$ for $N$ in the original formula and then solve for $k$.

$$t = \frac{1}{k}\ln\frac{N_0}{N}$$

$$t_{0.5} = \frac{1}{k}\ln\frac{N_0}{\frac{N_0}{2}}$$

$$t_{0.5} = \frac{1}{k}\ln 2$$

$$kt_{0.5} = \ln 2$$

$$k = \frac{\ln 2}{t_{0.5}}$$

b. Substitute the value of $k$ found in part a to introduce $t_{0.5}$ into the original formula.

$$t = \frac{1}{k}\ln\frac{N_0}{N}$$

$$t = \frac{t_{0.5}}{\ln 2}\ln\frac{N_0}{N}$$

$$\frac{t}{t_{0.5}}\ln 2 = \ln\frac{N_0}{N}$$

$$e^{\frac{t}{t_{0.5}}\ln 2} = \frac{N_0}{N}$$

$$e^{-\frac{t}{t_{0.5}}\ln 2} = \frac{N}{N_0}$$

$$N = N_0 e^{-\frac{t}{t_{0.5}}\ln 2} = N_0\left(2^{-\frac{t}{t_{0.5}}}\right)$$

## Rubric

a. 1 point for recognizing that at $t = t_{0.5}$, $N = \dfrac{N_0}{2}$; 1 point for correct answer

b. 1 point for substituting the answer from part a into the original formula; 1 point for a correct equation for $N$; 1 point for simplified answer (note that $N = N_0 e^{-\frac{t}{t_{0.5}} \ln 2}$ is an acceptable simplified answer, as it is a common way to represent this formula)

9. First, solve the given formula for $R$.

$$T^2 = \frac{4\pi^2}{GM} R^3$$

$$R^3 = \frac{GM}{4\pi^2} T^2$$

$$R = \sqrt[3]{\frac{GM}{4\pi^2} T^2}$$

Because Jupiter and Earth both orbit the same star, $M$ is the same for both of them. The period of Earth is 1 year, and the period of Jupiter is 11.86 years. Let $R_E$ represent the semi-major axis of Earth, and let $R_J$ represent the semi-major axis of Jupiter.

$$R_E = \sqrt[3]{\frac{GM}{4\pi^2}(1)^2}$$

$$= \sqrt[3]{\frac{GM}{4\pi^2}}$$

$$R_J = \sqrt[3]{\frac{GM}{4\pi^2}(11.86)^2}$$

$$= \left(\sqrt[3]{11.86^2}\right)\sqrt[3]{\frac{GM}{4\pi^2}}$$

Because the rightmost factor in this last equation gives the semi-major axis for Earth, you can make a direct comparison between Jupiter's semi-major axis and Earth's.

$$R_J = \left(\sqrt[3]{11.86^2}\right) R_E$$

$$\approx 5.2 R_E$$

So, Jupiter is roughly 5.2 times farther away from the Sun than Earth is.

## Rubric

1 point for rearranging the equation;
1 point for using $T = 1$ for Earth;
1 point for accurate work;
1 point for correct answer

# A.REI.1 Answers

1. A
2. A, D, F
3. Justification for step (2): Subtraction property of equality
   Justification for step (5): Power of a product property
   Justification for step (7): Product of powers property
   Justification for step (8): Division property of equality

**Rubric**

1 point for each answer

4.

$$\frac{5x^2+4x+3}{x^2+2x-1}=6 \qquad\qquad\qquad\text{Given}$$

$$\frac{5x^2+4x+3}{x^2+2x-1}(x^2+2x-1)=6(x^2+2x-1) \qquad\text{Multiplication property of equality}$$

$$5x^2+4x+3=6x^2+12x-6 \qquad\qquad\text{Distributive property}$$

$$5x^2+4x+3-(5x^2+4x+3)=6x^2+12x-6-(5x^2+4x+3) \qquad\text{Subtraction property of equality}$$

$$0=6x^2+12x-6-(5x^2+4x+3) \qquad\text{Additive inverse property}$$

$$0=6x^2+12x-6-5x^2-4x-3 \qquad\text{Distributive property}$$

$$0=x^2+8x-9 \qquad\qquad\qquad\text{Simplify.}$$

$$0=(x-1)(x+9) \qquad\qquad\qquad\text{Factor.}$$

$$0=x-1 \quad\text{or}\quad 0=x+9 \qquad\qquad\text{Zero product property}$$

$$0+1=x-1+1 \text{ or } 0-9=x+9-9 \qquad\text{Addition/subtraction prop. of equality}$$

$$1=x \qquad\text{or}\qquad -9=x \qquad\qquad\text{Simplify.}$$

**Rubric**

1 point for correct answer;
1 point for correct solution method;
2 points for appropriate justification of solution steps, especially regarding the properties of equality and the distributive property

---

5.

$$5 = 10\sqrt{1 - \frac{x^2}{a^2}}$$     Given

$$\frac{5}{10} = \frac{10}{10}\sqrt{1 - \frac{x^2}{a^2}}$$     Division property of equality

$$\frac{1}{2} = \sqrt{1 - \frac{x^2}{a^2}}$$     Simplify.

$$\left(\frac{1}{2}\right)^2 = \left(\sqrt{1 - \frac{x^2}{a^2}}\right)^2$$     Square both sides.

$$\frac{1}{4} = 1 - \frac{x^2}{a^2}$$     Definition of square root

$$\frac{1}{4} + \frac{x^2}{a^2} - \frac{1}{4} = 1 - \frac{x^2}{a^2} + \frac{x^2}{a^2} - \frac{1}{4}$$     Addition and subtraction properties of equality

$$\frac{x^2}{a^2} = \frac{3}{4}$$     Simplify.

$$\frac{x^2}{a^2} \cdot a^2 = \frac{3}{4} \cdot a^2$$     Multiplication property of equality

$$x^2 = \frac{3a^2}{4}$$     Simplify.

$$\sqrt{x^2} = \sqrt{\frac{3a^2}{4}}$$     Take the square root of both sides.

$$x = \sqrt{\frac{3a^2}{4}}$$     Definition of square root

$$x = \frac{\sqrt{3a^2}}{\sqrt{4}}$$     Power of a quotient property

$$x = \frac{\sqrt{3}\sqrt{a^2}}{\sqrt{4}}$$     Power of a product property

$$x = \frac{\sqrt{3}}{2}a$$     Definition of square root

### Rubric
1 point for reasonable solution process;
1 point for correct answer;
3 points for appropriate justification of solution steps

6. The time it takes for the team to run the race is equal to the sum of the runners' individual times (denoted $t_1$, $t_2$, $t_3$, and $t_4$). Since $t = \dfrac{d}{r}$ and all four distances are 100 meters, a rational equation can be created and solved to find the speeds. Let $r$ represent the speed of the two slower runners.

$$t = t_1 + t_2 + t_3 + t_4 \qquad \text{Given}$$

$$70 = \frac{100}{r} + \frac{100}{r} + \frac{100}{r+2} + \frac{100}{r+2} \qquad \text{Substitution property of equality}$$

$$70 = \frac{200}{r} + \frac{200}{r+2} \qquad \text{Simplify.}$$

$$70 = \frac{200}{r} \cdot \frac{r+2}{r+2} + \frac{200}{r+2} \cdot \frac{r}{r} \qquad \text{Identity property of multiplication}$$

$$70 = \frac{200(r+2)}{r(r+2)} + \frac{200r}{r(r+2)} \qquad \text{Rule for fraction multiplication}$$

$$70 = \frac{200r+400}{r^2+2r} + \frac{200r}{r^2+2r} \qquad \text{Distributive property}$$

$$70 = \frac{200r+400+200r}{r^2+2r} \qquad \text{Rule for fraction addition}$$

$$70 = \frac{400r+400}{r^2+2r} \qquad \text{Simplify.}$$

$$70(r^2+2r) = \frac{400r+400}{r^2+2r}(r^2+2r) \qquad \text{Multiplication property of equality}$$

$$70(r^2+2r) = 400r+400 \qquad \text{Simplify.}$$

$$70r^2+140r = 400r+400 \qquad \text{Distributive property}$$

$$70r^2+140r-(400r+400) = 400r+400-(400r+400) \qquad \text{Subtraction property of equality}$$

$$70r^2+140r-(400r+400) = 0 \qquad \text{Simplify.}$$

$$70r^2+140r-400r-400 = 0 \qquad \text{Distributive property}$$

$$70r^2-260r-400 = 0 \qquad \text{Simplify.}$$

$$r = \frac{-(-260) \pm \sqrt{(-260)^2 - 4(70)(-400)}}{2(70)} \qquad \text{Quadratic formula}$$

$$r \approx 4.9, -1.2 \qquad \text{Simplify.}$$

Since speed cannot be negative, $r \approx 4.9$ meters per second, so the speed of the two slower runners is about 4.9 meters per second. The two other runners run 2 meters per second faster, so their speed is about 6.9 meters per second.

**Rubric**
1 point for setting up the equation;
1 point for reasonable solution process;
1 point for correct answer;
3 points for appropriate justification of solution steps

# A.REI.2 Answers

1. B

2. D

3. A, B, D

4.

$$\sqrt{2x+1}+7 = x$$
$$\sqrt{2x+1} = x-7$$
$$2x+1 = (x-7)^2$$
$$2x+1 = x^2-14x+49$$
$$0 = x^2-16x+48$$
$$0 = (x-4)(x-12)$$
$$0 = x-4 \text{ or } 0 = x-12$$
$$x = 4 \qquad \text{or } x = 12$$

Check the apparent solution $x = 4$.

$$\sqrt{2(4)+1}+7 \overset{?}{=} 4$$
$$\sqrt{9}+7 \overset{?}{=} 4$$
$$3+7 \overset{?}{=} 4$$
$$10 \neq 4$$

Check the apparent solution $x = 12$.

$$\sqrt{2(12)+1}+7 \overset{?}{=} 12$$
$$\sqrt{25}+7 \overset{?}{=} 12$$
$$5+7 \overset{?}{=} 12$$
$$12 = 12$$

Since substituting 4 for $x$ in the equation results in a false statement, 4 is an extraneous solution. So, the only solution is 12.

## Rubric
0.5 point for each apparent solution; 1 point for recognizing the extraneous solution; 1 point for showing work

5.

$$\frac{2x}{5} = -4 + \frac{x-1}{x+2}$$
$$\left[\frac{2x}{5}\right]5(x+2) = \left[-4+\frac{x-1}{x+2}\right]5(x+2)$$
$$2x(x+2) = -20(x+2)+5(x-1)$$
$$2x^2+4x = -20x-40+5x-5$$
$$2x^2+19x+45 = 0$$
$$(x+5)(2x+9) = 0$$
$$x+5 = 0 \quad \text{or } 2x+9 = 0$$
$$x = -5 \text{ or} \qquad x = -\frac{9}{2}$$

The expression $\dfrac{x-1}{x+2}$ has an excluded value of $-2$.

Check the apparent solution $x = -5$.

$$\frac{2(-5)}{5} \overset{?}{=} -4+\frac{-5-1}{-5+2}$$
$$\frac{-10}{5} \overset{?}{=} -4+\frac{-6}{-3}$$
$$-2 \overset{?}{=} -4+2$$
$$-2 = -2$$

Check the apparent solution $x = -\dfrac{9}{2}$.

$$\frac{2\left(-\dfrac{9}{2}\right)}{5} \overset{?}{=} -4+\frac{-\dfrac{9}{2}-1}{-\dfrac{9}{2}+2}$$
$$\frac{-9}{5} \overset{?}{=} -4+\frac{-\dfrac{11}{2}}{-\dfrac{5}{2}}$$
$$-\frac{9}{5} \overset{?}{=} -4+\frac{11}{5}$$
$$-\frac{9}{5} = -\frac{9}{5}$$

Since both of the apparent solutions result in true statements and neither is the excluded value, there are no extraneous solutions. So, both $-5$ and $-\dfrac{9}{2}$ are solutions of the equation.

## Rubric

0.5 point for each apparent solution; 1 point for checking for extraneous solutions; 1 point for showing work

6. Solving the equation does indeed give $-2$ and $-10$ as the only *apparent* solutions, but they must be checked.

Substitute $-2$ for $x$ in the equation.

$$\sqrt{-8(-2)-16}-2 \overset{?}{=} -2$$
$$\sqrt{16-16}-2 \overset{?}{=} -2$$
$$\sqrt{0}-2 \overset{?}{=} -2$$
$$0-2 \overset{?}{=} -2$$
$$-2 = -2$$

Substitute $-10$ for $x$ in the equation.

$$\sqrt{-8(-10)-16}-2 \overset{?}{=} -10$$
$$\sqrt{80-16}-2 \overset{?}{=} -10$$
$$\sqrt{64}-2 \overset{?}{=} -10$$
$$8-2 \overset{?}{=} -10$$
$$6 \neq -10$$

A true statement occurs when $-2$ is substituted for $x$ in the equation, but a false statement occurs when $-10$ is substituted for $x$ in the equation (which means that $-10$ is an extraneous solution). So, Josie is incorrect, and $-2$ is the only solution of the equation.

## Rubric

1 point for answer; 2 points for justification

7. a.
$$\frac{6}{2-x}+\frac{6}{2+x}=3$$
$$\left[\frac{6}{2-x}+\frac{6}{2+x}\right](2-x)(2+x)=3(2-x)(2+x)$$
$$6(2+x)+6(2-x)=-3x^2+12$$
$$12+6x+12-6x=-3x^2+12$$
$$24=-3x^2+12$$
$$12=-3x^2$$
$$-4=x^2$$

Since the square of $x$ cannot equal a negative number, the equation has no solution.

b. Substitute 1 for $x$ to find the value of $g$.

$$\frac{6}{2-(1)}+\frac{6}{2+(1)}=g$$
$$6+2=g$$
$$8=g$$

c. Solve the equation $\dfrac{6}{2-x}+\dfrac{6}{2+x}=8$.

$$\frac{6}{2-x}+\frac{6}{2+x}=8$$
$$\left[\frac{6}{2-x}+\frac{6}{2+x}\right](2-x)(2+x)=8(2-x)(2+x)$$
$$6(2+x)+6(2-x)=-8x^2+32$$
$$12+6x+12-6x=-8x^2+32$$
$$24=-8x^2+32$$
$$-8=-8x^2$$
$$1=x^2$$
$$\pm\sqrt{1}=x$$
$$x=1 \text{ or } -1$$

The equation has a second apparent solution of $-1$. Substitute it into the equation to check it.

$$\frac{6}{2-(-1)}+\frac{6}{2+(-1)} \overset{?}{=} 8$$
$$2+6 \overset{?}{=} 8$$
$$8=8$$

Since $-1$ is not an extraneous solution, the equation has an additional solution of $-1$.

## Rubric

a. 2 points

b. 0.5 point for value of $g$; 0.5 point for work

c. 1 point for additional solution of $-1$; 1 point for verifying it is not an extraneous solution

8. Possible answer:

$$\frac{x}{x+6} = \frac{12}{x+4} - \frac{24}{x^2+10x+24}$$

Solving the rational equation gives the apparent solutions –4 and 12.

The apparent solution –4 is an extraneous solution of the equation because the expressions $\dfrac{12}{x+4}$ and

$\dfrac{24}{(x+6)(x+4)}$ are undefined when

$x = -4$.

**Rubric**

2 points for giving an equation with an extraneous solution; 1 point for solving the equation; 1 point for explaining why the extraneous solution occurs

9. Aaron should not have divided both sides of the equation by $x$ without specifying that $x \neq 0$ since division by 0 is undefined. If he had then considered the case $x = 0$ separately and substituted 0 for $x$ into the equation, he would have seen that 0 is a solution.

Alternatively, Aaron could have avoided "throwing away" 0 as a solution by rewriting $x^2 = x$ as $x^2 - x = 0$, factoring to get $x(x - 1) = 0$, and then applying the zero product property to get $x = 0$ and $x = 1$ as solutions (both of which check in the original equation).

**Rubric**

1 point for identifying Aaron's mistake; 1 point for each way of avoiding the mistake

# A.REI.4b Answers

1. C

2. A

3. C, D

4. a. $x = \pm 4$

   b. $x = \pm 6i$

   c. $x = \pm\sqrt{17}$

   d. $x = \pm i\sqrt{5}$

**Rubric**

0.5 point for each correct answer

5.
$$x^2 + 14x + 65 = -2$$
$$x^2 + 14x = -67$$
$$x^2 + 14x + 49 = -18$$
$$(x+7)^2 = -18$$
$$x + 7 = \pm\sqrt{-18}$$
$$x + 7 = \pm 3i\sqrt{2}$$
$$x = -7 \pm 3i\sqrt{2}$$

**Rubric**

1 point for correct solutions; 1 point for completing the square

6. a. Using the quadratic formula most easily solves the quadratic equation $3x^2 - 9x + 20 = 13$ as it is not factorable, the leading coefficient is not equal to 1, and the coefficient of the $x$-term is odd.

   b. Subtract 13 from both sides to put the equation in standard form and then use the quadratic formula to find the solutions.
   $$3x^2 - 9x + 20 = 13$$
   $$3x^2 - 9x + 7 = 0$$

$$x = \frac{-b \pm \sqrt{b^2 - 4ac}}{2a}$$

$$x = \frac{-(-9) \pm \sqrt{(-9)^2 - 4(3)(7)}}{2(3)}$$

$$= \frac{9 \pm \sqrt{81 - 84}}{6}$$

$$= \frac{9 \pm \sqrt{-3}}{6}$$

$$= \frac{3}{2} \pm \frac{\sqrt{3}}{6}i$$

**Rubric**

a. 1 point for a reasonable explanation

b. 1 point for correct solutions; 2 points for correct use of the method chosen in part a

7. First, rewrite the equation as a quadratic equation in standard form.
$$3x + 5 = \frac{8}{x}$$
$$x(3x + 5) = 8$$
$$3x^2 + 5x = 8$$
$$3x^2 + 5x - 8 = 0$$

Next, factor the equation to find the solutions.
$$3x^2 + 5x - 8 = 0$$
$$(3x + 8)(x - 1) = 0$$

So, $x = -\frac{8}{3}$ or $x = 1$.

**Rubric**

1 point for rewriting the equation as a quadratic equation in standard form;
1 point for correct solutions; 1 point for method of solution

**8. a.** The equation has two non-real solutions if the discriminant is negative.

$$b^2 - 4ac < 0$$
$$8^2 - 4(k)(11) < 0$$
$$64 - 44k < 0$$
$$-44k < -64$$
$$k > \frac{64}{44}$$
$$k > \frac{16}{11}$$

**b.** The equation has one real solution if the discriminant is zero. Since the discriminant is negative when $k > \frac{16}{11}$, it follows that the discriminant is zero when $k = \frac{16}{11}$.

**c.** The equation has two real solutions if the discriminant is positive. Since the discriminant is negative when $k > \frac{16}{11}$, it follows that the discriminant is positive when $k < \frac{16}{11}$.

**d.** The solutions of the equation can be found using the quadratic formula.

$$x = \frac{-b \pm \sqrt{b^2 - 4ac}}{2a}$$
$$x = \frac{-8 \pm \sqrt{8^2 - 4(k)(11)}}{2k}$$
$$= \frac{-8 \pm \sqrt{64 - 44k}}{2k}$$
$$= \frac{-8 \pm 2\sqrt{16 - 11k}}{2k}$$
$$= \frac{-4 \pm \sqrt{16 - 11k}}{k}$$

First, consider the values of $k$ from part a. You know that when $k > \frac{16}{11}$, the discriminant is negative. The solutions $x = \frac{-4 \pm \sqrt{16 - 11k}}{k}$ should be written with $i$ as directed.

$$x = \frac{-4 \pm \sqrt{16 - 11k}}{k}$$
$$= \frac{-4 \pm \sqrt{-(-16 + 11k)}}{k}$$
$$= \frac{-4 \pm \sqrt{-1}\sqrt{(11k - 16)}}{k}$$
$$= \frac{-4 \pm i\sqrt{11k - 16}}{k}$$
$$= -\frac{4}{k} \pm \frac{\sqrt{11k - 16}}{k}i$$

Next, consider the values of $k$ from part b. You know that when $k = \frac{16}{11}$, the discriminant is zero. Find the value of $x$ when $k = \frac{16}{11}$.

$$x = \frac{-4 \pm \sqrt{16 - 11k}}{k}$$
$$= \frac{-4 \pm 0}{k}$$
$$= -\frac{4}{k}$$
$$= -\frac{4}{\frac{16}{11}}$$
$$= -\frac{11}{4}$$

Finally, consider the values of $k$ from part c. You know that when $k < \frac{16}{11}$, the discriminant is positive. No rewriting of the solutions $x = \frac{-4 \pm \sqrt{16 - 11k}}{k}$ is warranted.

So, the solutions of the quadratic equation are as follows.

$$x = \begin{cases} \dfrac{-4 \pm \sqrt{16 - 11k}}{k} & \text{when } k < \dfrac{16}{11} \\ -\dfrac{11}{4} & \text{when } k = \dfrac{16}{11} \\ -\dfrac{4}{k} \pm \dfrac{\sqrt{11k - 16}}{k}i & \text{when } k > \dfrac{16}{11} \end{cases}$$

**Rubric**

a. 1 point

b. 0.5 point

c. 0.5 point

d. 1 point for correct solutions of the equation when $k < \dfrac{16}{11}$ and associated work; 1 point for correct solutions of the equation when $k = \dfrac{16}{11}$ and associated work; 1 point for correct solutions of the equation when $k > \dfrac{16}{11}$ and associated work

9. a. Solve the equation by taking a square root when $b = 0$ because the equation simply becomes $x^2 = 4$.

b. Solve the equation by factoring when $b = -3$ or $b = 3$ because once the equation is in standard form after subtracting 4 from both sides, the left side becomes factorable.

c. Solve the equation by completing the square or using the quadratic formula for all values of $b$ other than $b = 0$, $b = 3$, and $b = -3$ because once the equation is in standard form, $x^2 + bx - 4 = 0$, you can see that the discriminant is $b^2 - 4(1)(-4)$, or $b^2 + 16$, which has values that are not perfect squares when $b \neq 0$ and $b \neq \pm 3$. Values of $b^2 + 16$ that are not perfect squares result in irrational solutions that can only be obtained by completing the square or using the quadratic formula.

**Rubric**

a. 1 point for value of $b$; 1 point for explanation

b. 1 point for value of $b$; 1 point for explanation

c. 1 point for value of $b$; 1 point for explanation

# A.REI.6 Answers

1. A

2. D

3. C

4. Multiply the second equation in the given system by 2 to get $2x - 16y - 6z = 74$. Compare the transformed second equation with the third equation and note that $2x - 16y - 6z$ cannot equal both 74 and 75. So, the system has no solution.

**Rubric**

1 point for correct answer; 1 point for appropriate justification

5. Subtract 2 times the second equation from the first equation to eliminate $x$.

$$2x + 3y + z = 27$$
$$- 2(x + 5y - 3z = 52)$$
$$\overline{\qquad -7y + 7z = -77}$$

Then add 3 times the second equation to the third equation to eliminate $x$.

$$3(x + 5y - 3z = 52)$$
$$+ \; -3x + y + 2x = -16$$
$$\overline{\qquad 16y - 7z = 140}$$

Add the two equations in $y$ and $z$ to eliminate $z$. Then solve for $y$.

$$-7y + 7z = -77$$
$$+ \; 16y - 7z = 140$$
$$\overline{\qquad 9y = 63}$$
$$y = 7$$

Use this value for $y$ and one of the equations in $y$ and $z$ to solve for $z$.

$$-7y + 7z = -77$$
$$-7(7) + 7z = -77$$
$$-49 + 7z = -77$$
$$7z = -28$$
$$z = -4$$

Use the values for $y$ and $z$ and one of the given equations to solve for $x$.

$$2x + 3y + z = 27$$
$$2x + 3(7) + (-4) = 27$$
$$2x + 17 = 27$$
$$2x = 10$$
$$x = 5$$

So, the solution is $x = 5$, $y = 7$, $z = -4$.

**Rubric**

1 point for $x$ and associated work;
1 point for $y$ and associated work;
1 point for $z$ and associated work

6. a. The system has infinitely many solutions because the third equation is a linear combination of the first two. Subtract the second equation from 2 times the first equation to get the third equation.

   b. Subtract 5 times the second equation from 7 times the first equation to eliminate $y$.

$$7(3x + 5y - 2z = -7)$$
$$- \; 5(-2x + 7y + 6z = -3)$$
$$\overline{\qquad 31x - 44z = -34}$$

This equation can be used to express $x$ in terms of $z$.

$$31x - 44z = -34$$
$$31x = 44z - 34$$
$$x = \frac{44z - 34}{31}$$

Add the third equation to 4 times the second equation to eliminate $x$. Solve this equation for $y$ in terms of $z$.

$$4(-2x + 7y + 6z = -3)$$
$$+ \; 8x + 3y - 10z = -11$$
$$\overline{\qquad 31y + 14z = -23}$$
$$31y = -14z - 23$$
$$y = \frac{-14z - 23}{31}$$

So, the solution of the given system of equations is $x = \dfrac{44z - 34}{31}$, $y = \dfrac{-14z - 23}{31}$, and $z = z$.

**Rubric**

a. 1 point

b. 1 point for $x$ in terms of $z$ and associated work; 1 point for $y$ in terms of $z$ and associated work

7. Let $a$ be the number of apples sold, $b$ be the number of bananas sold, and $c$ be the number of oranges (citrus) sold. Three equations can be generated from the given information: one for total fruit sold, one for revenue, and one expressing $b$ in terms of $c$.

$$\begin{cases} a + b + c = 50 \\ 0.75a + 0.5b + 0.75c = 33.50 \\ b = 2c \end{cases}$$

Use the third equation to substitute $2c$ for $b$ in the first equation.

$$a + b + c = 50$$
$$a + 2c + c = 50$$
$$a + 3c = 50$$

Also use the third equation to substitute $2c$ for $b$ in the second equation.

$$0.75a + 0.5b + 0.75c = 33.50$$
$$0.75a + 0.5(2c) + 0.75c = 33.50$$
$$0.75a + c + 0.75c = 33.50$$
$$0.75a + 1.75c = 33.50$$

Multiply the equation $a + 3c = 50$ by 0.75 and subtract the equation $0.75a + 1.75c = 33.50$ from it.

$$\begin{array}{r} 0.75(a + 3c = 50) \\ - (0.75a + 1.75c = 33.50) \\ \hline 0.5c = 4 \\ c = 8 \end{array}$$

Use this value for $c$ and the equation $a + 3c = 50$ to solve for $a$.

$$a + 3c = 50$$
$$a + 3(8) = 50$$
$$a + 24 = 50$$
$$a = 26$$

So, 26 apples were sold at the fruit sale.

**Rubric**

1 point for each correct initial equation;
1 point for appropriate solution process;
1 point for correct answer

8. Let $c$ be the number of hours that Carlotta worked, let $j$ be the number of hours that James worked, and let $m$ be the number of hours that Melissa worked. Three equations can be generated from the given information: one for total number of hours worked, one for total pastries decorated, and one for total wages earned.

$$\begin{cases} c + j + m = 96 \\ 12c + 11j + 7m = 1016 \\ 11c + 10j + 8m = 960 \end{cases}$$

Multiply the first equation by 11 and subtract the third equation from it to eliminate $c$.

$$\begin{array}{r} 11(c + j + m = 96) \\ - (11c + 10j + 8m = 960) \\ \hline j + 3m = 96 \end{array}$$

Multiply the first equation by 12 and subtract the second equation from it to eliminate $c$ again.

$$\begin{array}{r} 12(c + j + m = 96) \\ - (12c + 11j + 7m = 1016) \\ \hline j + 5m = 136 \end{array}$$

Subtract the equation $j + 3m = 96$ from the equation $j + 5m = 136$ to eliminate $j$ and solve for $m$.

$$j + 5m = 136$$
$$\underline{- (j + 3m = 96)}$$
$$2m = 40$$
$$m = 20$$

Use this value for $m$ and the equation $j + 5m = 136$ to solve for $j$.

$$j + 5m = 136$$
$$j + 5(20) = 136$$
$$j + 100 = 136$$
$$j = 36$$

Use one of the original equations and the values of $m$ and $j$ to find $c$.

$$c + j + m = 96$$
$$c + 36 + 20 = 96$$
$$c + 56 = 96$$
$$c = 40$$

So, Carlotta worked 40 hours, James worked 36 hours, and Melissa worked 20 hours that week.

**Rubric**
1 point for each correct initial equation; 1 point for appropriate solution process; 1 point for each correct answer

9. Let $a$ be the price of an armchair, let $s$ be the price of a side chair, and let $t$ be the price of a table. Three equations can be generated from the given information: one for each listed set.

$$\begin{cases} 2a + 4s + t = 940 \\ 4s + t = 740 \\ 4a + 2s + t = 1020 \end{cases}$$

Multiply the first equation by 2 and subtract the third equation from it to eliminate $a$.

$$2(2a + 4s + t = 940)$$
$$\underline{- (4a + 2s + t = 1020)}$$
$$6s + t = 860$$

Subtract the second equation from the equation $6s + t = 860$ to eliminate $t$ and solve for $s$.

$$6s + t = 860$$
$$\underline{- (4s + t = 740)}$$
$$2s = 120$$
$$s = 60$$

Use this value for $s$ and the equation $4s + t = 740$ to solve for $t$.

$$4s + t = 740$$
$$4(60) + t = 740$$
$$240 + t = 740$$
$$t = 500$$

Use the equation $2a + 4s + t = 940$ and the values of $s$ and $t$ to find $a$.

$$2a + 4s + t = 940$$
$$2a + 4(60) + 500 = 940$$
$$2a + 740 = 940$$
$$2a = 200$$
$$a = 100$$

So, an armchair costs $100, a side chair costs $60, and a table costs $500. The table is a necessary $500 to spend. With the remaining $400, a set of 6 side chairs or a set of 4 armchairs could be bought. (Combinations of armchairs and side chairs could also be bought, although chairs are typically used in pairs in a dining room, so a combination of 2 armchairs and 2 side chairs is more common than, say, a combination of 2 armchairs and 3 side chairs.)

**Rubric**
1 point for each correct initial equation; 1 point for appropriate solution process; 1 point for each correct answer; 1 point for a reasonable purchasing plan for the budget provided

# A.REI.7 Answers

1. B

2. C

3. A, B

4.

$$2x + y = 4$$
$$y = -2x + 4$$

$$\frac{x^2}{4} + \frac{y^2}{16} = 1$$

$$\frac{x^2}{4} + \frac{(-2x+4)^2}{16} = 1$$

$$\frac{x^2}{4} + \frac{4x^2 - 16x + 16}{16} = 1$$

$$16 \cdot \frac{x^2}{4} + 16 \cdot \frac{4x^2 - 16x + 16}{16} = 16 \cdot 1$$

$$4x^2 + 4x^2 - 16x + 16 = 16$$

$$8x^2 - 16x = 0$$

$$8x(x - 2) = 0$$

$$x = 0 \text{ or } 2$$

Substitute 0 for $x$ in $2x + y = 4$.

$$2(0) + y = 4$$
$$y = 4$$

Substitute 2 for $x$ in $2x + y = 4$.

$$2(2) + y = 4$$
$$4 + y = 4$$
$$y = 0$$

The points of intersection are (0, 4) and (2, 0).

**Rubric**

1 point for each correct point of intersection; 2 points for showing work

5.

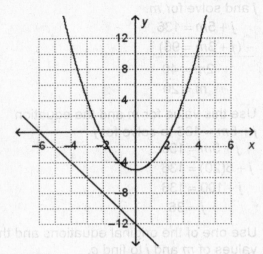

There are no solutions.

**Rubric**

0.5 point for each accurately graphed equation; 1 point for stating there are no solutions

6.

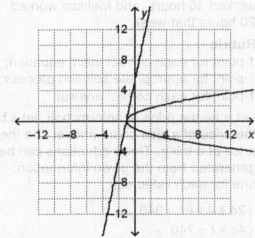

The solution of the system is (−1, 0).

**Rubric**

1 point for each accurately graphed equation; 1 point for reasonable answer estimate

7. Possible answer: Terrell knew he made a mistake because he only found one solution of the system, but his graph showed two points of intersection.

Terrell's mistake was only adding the square root when applying the quadratic formula instead of using $\pm$.

$$x^2 + 4x - 21 = -2x - 5$$
$$x^2 + 6x - 16 = 0$$
$$x = \frac{-6 \pm \sqrt{36 - 4(1)(-16)}}{2}$$
$$= \frac{-6 \pm \sqrt{100}}{2}$$
$$= \frac{-6 \pm 10}{2}$$
$$= 2 \text{ or } -8$$

$$-2(2) - 5 = -9$$
$$-2(-8) - 5 = 11$$

The solutions of the system of equations are (2, −9) and (−8, 11).

**Rubric**

1 point for a reasonable explanation of how Terrell knew he made a mistake; 1 point for correctly identifying Terrell's mistake; 1 point for each solution with accurate work

# A.REI.11* Answers

1. C

2. B

3. B, C, E

4. The solution occurs between $x = 2$ and $x = 3$ because prior to $x = 3$, $f(x) > g(x)$. At $x = 3$ and beyond, $f(x) < g(x)$.

   To decide whether $x = 2$ or $x = 3$ is the more accurate approximation, evaluate the functions at $x = 2.5$.

   $$f(x) = -|x - 2| + 5$$
   $$f(2.5) = -|2.5 - 2| + 5$$
   $$= 4.5$$
   $$g(x) = 2\sqrt{x} + 1$$
   $$g(2.5) = 2\sqrt{2.5} + 1$$
   $$\approx 4.16$$

   Since $f(2.5) > g(2.5)$, the solution lies in the range $2.5 < x < 3$. So, $x = 3$ is the most accurate integer approximation of the solution of $f(x) = g(x)$.

   **Rubric**
   1 point for correct answer; 1 point for reasonable justification

5.

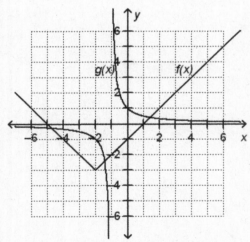

   To the nearest 0.5 unit, the solutions of the equation $f(x) = g(x)$ are $x = -4.5$, $x = -1.5$, and $x = 1.5$.

**Rubric**
1 point for correct graph of $f(x)$; 1 point for correct graph of $g(x)$; 1 point for acceptable solutions

6. The points where the graphs of $P_A(t)$ and $P_B(t)$ intersect are the points where business A and business B are generating the same amount of annual profit at the same time. The points of intersection occur at $t = 0$ years and $t \approx 8.5$ years.

**Rubric**
1 point for the significance of the points; 1 point for accurate approximations

7.

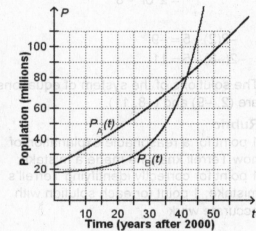

The intersection of the two graphs occurs at approximately $t = 42$, so it will take about 42 years after 2000, or until 2042, for country B to have the same population as country A.

**Rubric**
1 point for each graph; 2 points for an appropriate approximation

# F.IF.4* Answers

1. C

2. A, D, H

3. a. There are 5 billion atoms of carbon-14 in the sample at time $t = 0$.

   b. The number of atoms of carbon-14 in the sample approaches 0 as $t$ approaches positive infinity.

   c. 5.73 thousand years, or 5730 years

   **Rubric**

   1 point for each part

4. a. $P(n)$ is always decreasing. This implies that the more times a number cube is rolled, the less likely it is that every roll is a 5.

   b. As $n$ approaches infinity, $P(n)$ approaches zero. Since $P(n)$ approaches zero asymptotically, no matter how many times the number cube is rolled, it is always possible, but unlikely, that every roll will be a 5.

   **Rubric**

   a. 1 point for answer; 1 point for a reasonable explanation of the significance

   b. 1 point for answer; 1 point for a reasonable explanation of the significance

   c. 1 point for answer; 1 point for a reasonable explanation of the significance

5. a. $V(t)$ is increasing for $0 < t < 3.5$ and $13 < t < 18$. $V(t)$ is decreasing for $3.5 < t < 13$.

   b. The value of the portfolio increased during the first 3.5 months, and then the value decreased until the 13th month, at which point the value began to increase again.

   c. A local maximum occurs at approximately (3.5, 2.25), and a local minimum occurs at approximately (13, 0.75).

   d. The local maximum indicates that during this period, the value of the portfolio reached a peak of about $2,250,000 after about 3.5 months before losing value. The local minimum indicates that during this period, the value of the portfolio decreased to about $750,000 after about 13 months before beginning to regain value.

   e. The fact that the function is always positive over this period indicates that the portfolio always had some value. This makes sense because the portfolio can only lose all its value; the portfolio cannot have negative value. In this aspect, the model is appropriate.

   **Rubric**

   a. 1 point for correct intervals

   b. 1 point for appropriate explanation of significance

   c. 0.5 point for correct local maximum; 0.5 point for correct local minimum

   d. 1 point for appropriate explanation of significance

   e. 1 point for noting value is always nonnegative; 1 point for stating model is appropriate

# F.IF.5* Answers

1. B

2. A

3. D

4. B, C, G

5. The domain of this function consists of all whole numbers. It is not possible to flip a negative number of coins or a fractional number of a coin. It is, however, possible to flip 0 coins and get a combination of 0 heads and 0 tails.

   The graph of $C(n)$ is discrete. Since the domain consists only of whole numbers, the graph would consist of isolated points, making the graph discrete.

   **Rubric**

   1 point for correct domain; 1 point for appropriate explanation; 1 point for discrete; 1 point for appropriate explanation

6. The domain of $h(t)$ is $t \geq 0$, and the range is $h(t) \geq 0$.

   The domain allows for the values of $t$ to increase without bound, but plants do not live forever. The model is not appropriate for values of $t$ greater than the normal lifespan of the plant.

   **Rubric**

   1 point for correct domain; 1 point for correct range; 1 point for explaining the practical limit on the domain

7. The domain of $N(t)$ is $t \geq 0$, and the range is $10 \leq N(t) < 1000$.

   The graph of $N(t)$ approaches 1000 asymptotically. This implies that not all of the inhabitants hear the story no matter how much time passes, which is highly unlikely. For practical purposes, the graph suggests that the domain is actually $0 \leq t \leq 10$.

   **Rubric**

   1 point for the correct domain; 1 point for the correct range; 2 points for a reasonable explanation why the model is not appropriate

8. The logarithmic function is defined for arguments greater than 0, so the domain of $P_{dB}(P)$ is $P > 0$. The range is $-\infty < P_{dB}(P) < \infty$.

   For $0 < P < 20$, which are pressures of sounds too faint to be heard by humans, the function values are negative. For $P > 20$, which are pressures of sounds that humans can hear, the function values are positive. So, on the decibel scale, inaudible sounds are represented by negative decibels and audible sounds are represented by positive decibels.

   **Rubric**

   1 point for correct domain; 1 point for correct range; 2 points for a reasonable interpretation

# F.IF.6* Answers

1. D
2. D
3. A, C, F
4. F
5. B
6. C
7. H
8. A
9. D

10. $V(3) = \left(\dfrac{6-\pi}{6}\right)3^3 \qquad V(2) = \left(\dfrac{6-\pi}{6}\right)2^3$

$\qquad\quad = \left(\dfrac{6-\pi}{6}\right)27 \qquad\quad = \left(\dfrac{6-\pi}{6}\right)8$

$\qquad\quad = 27 - \dfrac{9}{2}\pi \qquad\qquad = 8 - \dfrac{4}{3}\pi$

$\dfrac{V(3)-V(2)}{3-2} = \dfrac{\left(27 - \dfrac{9}{2}\pi\right) - \left(8 - \dfrac{4}{3}\pi\right)}{1}$

$\qquad\qquad\quad = 27 - \dfrac{9}{2}\pi - 8 + \dfrac{4}{3}\pi$

$\qquad\qquad\quad = 19 - \dfrac{19}{6}\pi$

$\qquad\qquad\quad \approx 9$

The average rate of change of $V(d)$ over the interval $2 \le d \le 3$ is about 9 cubic feet per foot.

**Rubric**
1 point for correct rate of change;
1 point for supporting work

11. $\dfrac{h(4)-h(0)}{4-0} \approx \dfrac{85-5}{4}$

$\qquad\qquad\quad = 20$ meters per minute

$\dfrac{h(8)-h(4)}{8-4} \approx \dfrac{5-85}{4}$

$\qquad\qquad\quad = -20$ meters per minute

The average rate of change represents the passenger's vertical velocity. The average rate of change over the interval $0 \le t \le 4$ tells you that the passenger is ascending at an average speed of 20 meters per minute for the first half of a rotation. The average rate of change over the interval $4 \le t \le 8$ tells you that the passenger is descending at an average speed of 20 meters per minute for the second half of a rotation.

**Rubric**
1 point for each estimated average rate of change; 1 point for a reasonable interpretation

12. On the interval $6 \le a \le 10$, the average rate of change is:

$\dfrac{h(10)-h(6)}{10-6} \approx \dfrac{15.5-13}{4}$

$\qquad\qquad\quad \approx 0.6$ inch per year

The average rate of change represents the average increase in the recommended chair seat height as a child's age increases by 1 year between ages 6 and 10.

**Rubric**
1 point for average rate of change;
1 point for a reasonable interpretation

13. a. On the interval $0 \le x \le 4$: average rate of change $= \dfrac{f(4)-f(0)}{4-0} = \dfrac{4^2-0^2}{4} = \dfrac{16}{4} = 4$

On the subinterval $0 \le x \le 2$: average rate of change $= \dfrac{f(2)-f(0)}{2-0} = \dfrac{2^2-0^2}{2} = \dfrac{4}{2} = 2$

On the subinterval $2 \le x \le 4$: average rate of change $= \dfrac{f(4)-f(2)}{4-2} = \dfrac{4^2-2^2}{2} = \dfrac{12}{2} = 6$

The mean of the average rates of change on the two subintervals is $\dfrac{2+6}{2} = 4$, which agrees with the average rate of change on the interval.

b. Possible answer: Let $b = 1$.

On the subinterval $0 \le x \le 1$: average rate of change $= \dfrac{f(1) - f(0)}{1 - 0} = \dfrac{1^2 - 0^2}{1 - 0} = \dfrac{1}{1} = 1$

On the subinterval $1 \le x \le 4$: average rate of change $= \dfrac{f(4) - f(1)}{4 - 1} = \dfrac{4^2 - 1^2}{4 - 1} = \dfrac{15}{3} = 5$

The mean of the average rates of change on the two subintervals is $\dfrac{1 + 5}{2} = 3$, which does not agree with the average rate of change on the interval.

c. Modified conjecture: The average rate of change of a function $f(x)$ defined for all $x$ on the interval $a \le x \le c$ is equal to the mean of the average rates of change of $f(x)$ on the subintervals $a \le x \le b$ and $b \le x \le c$, where $b = \dfrac{a + c}{2}$.

Proof:

On the interval $a \le x \le c$: average rate of change $= \dfrac{f(c) - f(a)}{c - a}$

On the subinterval $a \le x \le \dfrac{a + c}{2}$:

average rate of change $= \dfrac{f\left(\dfrac{a+c}{2}\right) - f(a)}{\dfrac{a+c}{2} - a} = \dfrac{f\left(\dfrac{a+c}{2}\right) - f(a)}{\dfrac{c-a}{2}}$

On the subinterval $\dfrac{a + c}{2} \le x \le c$:

average rate of change $= \dfrac{f(c) - f\left(\dfrac{a+c}{2}\right)}{c - \dfrac{a+c}{2}} = \dfrac{f(c) - f\left(\dfrac{a+c}{2}\right)}{\dfrac{c-a}{2}}$

The mean of the average rates of change on the two subintervals is:

$$\dfrac{\dfrac{f\left(\dfrac{a+c}{2}\right) - f(a)}{\dfrac{c-a}{2}} + \dfrac{f(c) - f\left(\dfrac{a+c}{2}\right)}{\dfrac{c-a}{2}}}{2} = \dfrac{\dfrac{f(c) - f(a)}{\dfrac{c-a}{2}}}{2} = \dfrac{f(c) - f(a)}{c - a}$$

This agrees with the average rate of change on the interval.

**Rubric**

a. 1 point for correctly showing that Erica's conjecture is true in this case

b. 2 points for providing a value for $b$ for which the conjecture is false for the function and interval given in part a and for showing that it is false

c. 3 points for correctly modifying the conjecture and proving the modified conjecture

# F.IF.7b* Answers

1. C

2. C

3. B, C

4. a.

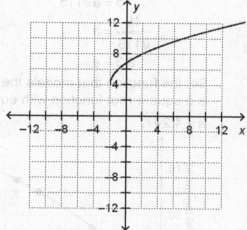

b. The domain of the function is all real numbers greater than or equal to −2. The range of the function is all real numbers greater than or equal to 4.

**Rubric**

a. 1 point

b. 1 point for domain; 1 point for range

5. a.

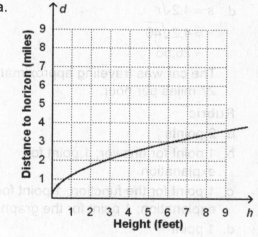

b. Possible answer:

The point (6, 2.9) is approximately on the graph. This point means that for a person whose eye level is 6 feet above the ground, the horizon that the person sees is about 2.9 miles away.

**Rubric**

a. 1 point

b. 1 point for locating a point on the graph; 1 point for interpretation

6.

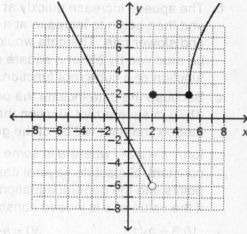

The domain of the function is all real numbers. The range of the function is all real numbers greater than −6. The graph intersects the x-axis at $x = -1$ and the y-axis at $y = -2$.

**Rubric**

1 point for each correctly graphed piece; 0.5 point each for domain, range, and intercepts

**7. a.**

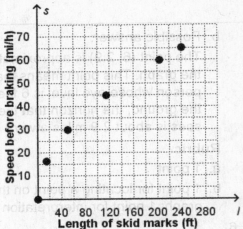

**b.** The speeds increase quickly at first and then begin to increase at a slower and slower rate. The data would best be modeled by either a square root function or a cube root function.

**c.** Because the data include the point $(0, 0)$, a square root function that models the data will be of the general form $s = a\sqrt{\ell}$, where $a$ is some constant. Substitute several data points into the general equation to see if the value of $a$ is indeed constant.

$$16.3 = a\sqrt{15} \qquad\qquad 30 = a\sqrt{51}$$
$$\frac{16.3}{\sqrt{15}} = a \qquad\qquad \frac{30}{\sqrt{51}} = a$$
$$4.2 \approx a \qquad\qquad 4.2 \approx a$$

$$45 = a\sqrt{115}$$
$$\frac{45}{\sqrt{115}} = a$$
$$4.2 \approx a$$

Similarly, a cube root function that models the data will be of the general form $s = a\sqrt[3]{\ell}$, where $a$ is some constant. Substitute several data points into the general equation to see if the value of $a$ is indeed constant.

$$16.3 = a\sqrt[3]{15} \qquad\qquad 30 = a\sqrt[3]{51}$$
$$\frac{16.3}{\sqrt[3]{15}} = a \qquad\qquad \frac{30}{\sqrt[3]{51}} = a$$
$$6.6 \approx a \qquad\qquad 8.1 \approx a$$

$$45 = a\sqrt[3]{115}$$
$$\frac{45}{\sqrt[3]{115}} = a$$
$$9.3 \approx a$$

So, the function that models the data is a square root function with equation $s = 4.2\sqrt{\ell}$.

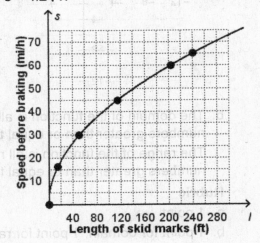

**d.**
$$s = 4.2\sqrt{\ell}$$
$$= 4.2\sqrt{40}$$
$$\approx 26.56$$

The car was traveling approximately 27 miles per hour.

**Rubric**

a. 2 points

b. 1 point for answer; 1 point for explanation

c. 1 point for the function; 1 point for explanation; 1 point for the graph

d. 1 point

# F.IF.7c* Answers

1. B

2. B

3. A, D, E

4. $p(x) = -x^3 - x^2 + 16x + 16$
$$= -(x^3 + x^2 - 16x - 16)$$
$$= [x^2(x+1) - 16(x+1)]$$
$$= -(x^2 - 16)(x+1)$$
$$= -(x-4)(x+4)(x+1)$$

The zeros of $p(x)$ are $-4$, $-1$, and 4.

As $x$ approaches $-\infty$, $p(x)$ approaches $\infty$. As $x$ approaches $\infty$, $p(x)$ approaches $-\infty$.

Besides plotting the points where the graph crosses the $x$-axis (as determined by the zeros), it may be helpful to plot these additional points: $(0, 16)$ and $(2, 36)$.

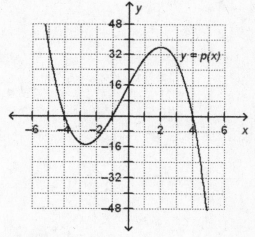

### Rubric
1 point for the correct zeros;
1 point for the correct end behavior;
2 points for the correct graph

5. a. Solving $2w + 2\ell = 20$ for $\ell$ gives $\ell = 10 - w$. So, the base of the pyramid is $w$ cm by $10 - w$ cm. The height is $\frac{3}{5}w(10-w)$.

$$V(w) = \frac{1}{3}w(10-w)\left(\frac{3}{5}w(10-w)\right)$$
$$= \frac{1}{5}w^4 - 4w^3 + 20w^2$$

b. The width $w$ must be positive, so $w > 0$. The length $10 - w$ must also be positive, so $10 - w > 0$ or $w < 10$. So, the domain is $0 < w < 10$.

c.

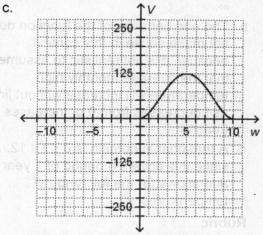

d. The maximum value of $V(w)$ on the domain $0 < w < 10$ is 125 at $w = 5$. So, the maximum volume of the pyramid is 125 cm³.

e. As $w$ approaches 0, $V(w)$ approaches 0. As $w$ approaches 10, $V(w)$ approaches 0. The volume of the pyramid approaches 0 as the values of $w$ approach the endpoints of the domain.

### Rubric
a. 1 point
b. 1 point
c. 2 points
d. 1 point
e. 1 point

6. a.

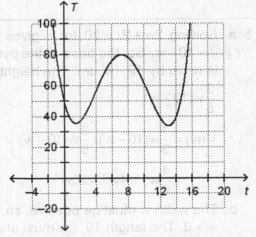

As $t$ approaches $\infty$, $T(t)$ approaches $\infty$.
As $t$ approaches $-\infty$, $T(t)$ approaches $\infty$.

b. The end behavior of the function does not make sense in this context because it is not realistic to assume that the average monthly high temperature will increase without limit as $t$ decreases from 0 or increases from 14.

c. A reasonable domain is $0 \le t \le 12$, since this covers a period of 1 year and allows for the full range of temperatures.

**Rubric**

a. 2 points for the graph;
   2 points for the end behavior

b. 2 points for answer and explanation

c. 2 points for domain and explanation

# F.IF.7e* Answers

1. B
2. D
3. C
4. C
5.

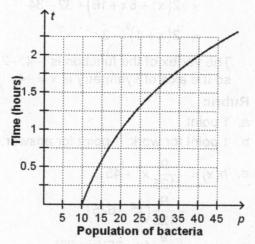

**Population of bacteria**

The *p*-intercept is 10, which is the initial population of bacteria.

**Rubric**
1 point for the graph;
1 point for the intercept;
1 point for a reasonable interpretation

6.

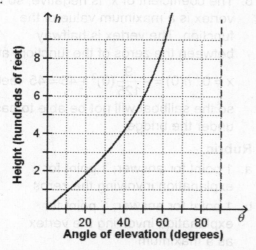

**Angle of elevation (degrees)**

There is a vertical asymptote at $\theta = 90°$. This means that no matter how tall a building is, the angle of elevation from Lenny's eyes to the top of the building can never reach 90°.

The function values increase extremely rapidly near an asymptote. For example, an angle of elevation of 80° corresponds to a height of nearly 3000 feet, and an angle of elevation of 85° corresponds to a height of over a mile.

**Rubric**
1 point for the graph; 1 point for the asymptote; 1 point for a reasonable explanation

7. a. The domain of $V(t)$ is $t \geq 0$. The range is $0 < V(t) \leq 31$.

b.

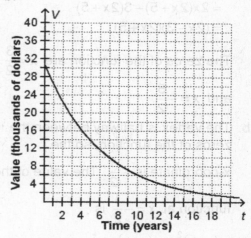

**Time (years)**

c. The *V*-intercept is 31. This represents the initial value of the forklift, $31,000.

d. There is no *t*-intercept because the graph of $V(t)$ approaches, but does not cross, the *t*-axis.

e. The graph would end at the point where $V(t) = 2$, which is approximately where $t = 17$. So, the forklift's useful life to the business is about 17 years.

**Rubric**
a. 1 point
b. 1 point
c. 1 point for the *V*-intercept;
1 point for the interpretation
d. 1 point
e. 1 point for describing change to graph;
1 point for length of useful life

# F.IF.8a Answers

1. B
2. B
3. B, C, E
4. a. False
   b. True
   c. False
   d. True
   e. True
5. a.
$$f(x) = 4x^2 + 4x - 15$$
$$= 4x^2 + 10x - 6x - 15$$
$$= 2x(2x+5) - 3(2x+5)$$
$$= (2x-3)(2x+5)$$

The zeros of the function are $x = \dfrac{3}{2}$

and $x = -\dfrac{5}{2}$.

   b. The vertex is halfway between the zeros of the function, so the

$x$-coordinate is $-\dfrac{1}{2}$. The value of the

function at $x = -\dfrac{1}{2}$ is

$$4\left(-\dfrac{1}{2}\right)^2 + 4\left(-\dfrac{1}{2}\right) - 15 = -16.$$

The vertex of $f(x)$ is $\left(-\dfrac{1}{2}, -16\right)$. The

coefficient of $x^2$ is positive, so the parabola opens up, and the vertex is the minimum value.

**Rubric**

   a. 1 point for factoring; 0.5 point for each zero
   b. 1 point for coordinates of the vertex; 1 point for stating that the vertex is a minimum; 1 point for explanation

6. a. Miguel is correct in saying that the function has no $x$-intercepts. However, the axis of symmetry can still be found by completing the square and finding the vertex. The axis of symmetry passes through the vertex.

   b. Complete the square:
$$f(x) = -2x^2 - 16x - 34$$
$$= -2\left(x^2 + 8x\right) - 34$$
$$= -2\left(x^2 + 8x + 16 - 16\right) - 34$$
$$= -2\left(x^2 + 8x + 16\right) + 32 - 34$$
$$= -2(x+4)^2 - 2$$

The vertex of the function is $(-4, -2)$, so the axis of symmetry is $x = -4$.

**Rubric**

   a. 1 point
   b. 1 point for work; 1 point for answer

7. a. $h(x) = -\dfrac{9}{125}x^2 + 45$
$$= -\dfrac{9}{125}\left(x^2 - 625\right)$$
$$= -\dfrac{9}{125}(x - 25)(x + 25)$$

The zeros of the function occur where the sides of the arch are at the water level. They are 25 feet to the left and right of the center of the bridge, so the bridge is 50 feet long.

   b. The coefficient of $x^2$ is negative, so the vertex is a maximum value of the function. The vertex is halfway between the zeros of the function, at

$x = 0$. $h(0) = -\dfrac{9}{125}(0)^2 + 45 = 45$ feet,

so the sailboat will not be able to pass under the bridge.

**Rubric**

   a. 1 point for answer; 1 point for explanation involving the zeros
   b. 1 point for answer; 1 point for explanation involving the vertex as a maximum

# F.IF.8b Answers

1. A

2. B

3. A, C, E, F, H

4. a. Not equivalent
   b. Equivalent
   c. Equivalent
   d. Not equivalent
   e. Equivalent
   f. Not equivalent

5. a. $P(t) = 3.98(1.02)^t$
   $= 3.98(1 + 0.02)^t$
   b. The value of $r$ is 0.02. This means that the population increases by 2% annually.

   **Rubric**
   a. 1 point
   b. 1 point for answer; 1 point for interpretation

6. $g(x) = 200\left(4^{x-1}\right)$
   $= 200\left(4^x \cdot 4^{-1}\right)$
   $= 200\left(\dfrac{4^x}{4}\right)$
   $= \dfrac{1}{4}\left(200\left(4^x\right)\right)$
   $= \dfrac{1}{4}\left(f(x)\right)$

   The function values of $g(x)$ are $\dfrac{1}{4}$ of the corresponding values of $f(x)$.

   **Rubric**
   2 points for work transforming $g(x)$; 1 point for answer

7. a. $V(t) = 1500(1.035)^t$
   $= 1500(1 + 0.035)^t$
   The annual interest rate is 3.5%.

   b. $V(t) = 1500(1.035)^t$
   $= 1500\left(1.035^5\right)^{\frac{t}{5}}$
   $\approx 1500(1.19)^{\frac{t}{5}}$
   The interest rate over 5 years is about 19%.

   **Rubric**
   a. 1 point
   b. 1 point for answer; 1 point for appropriate work

8. a. $B(t) = 850\left(1.04\right)^t$
   $= 850(1 + 0.04)^t$
   The annual interest rate is 4%.

   b. $B(t) = 850\left(1.04\right)^t$
   $= 850\left(1.04^{\frac{1}{12}}\right)^{12t}$
   $\approx 850(1.0033)^{12t}$
   The monthly interest rate is approximately 0.33%.

   c. Rebecca's account will have a larger balance after 6 months. Since $0.35 > 0.33$, Rebecca's account earns a greater amount of interest each month.

   **Rubric**
   a. 1 point for rewriting the function; 1 point for answer
   b. 1 point for rewriting the function; 1 point for answer
   c. 1 point for answer; 1 point for explanation

# F.IF.9 Answers

1. B

2. C

3. A, C, D, F

4. Since the graph of $f(x) = x^2 - 4x - 1$ is a parabola that opens up, the minimum value is the $y$-coordinate of the vertex. Complete the square to determine the coordinates of the vertex.

$$f(x) = x^2 - 4x - 1$$
$$= (x^2 - 4x + 4) - 1 - 4$$
$$= (x - 2)^2 - 5$$

The coordinates of the vertex are $(2, -5)$, so the minimum value is $-5$.

A cosine function whose graph has an amplitude of 4.5 and the $x$-axis as its midline has a minimum value of $-4.5$.

Since $-5 < -4.5$, $f(x) = x^2 - 4x - 1$ has the lesser minimum value.

**Rubric**

1 point for each minimum value; 1 point for identifying the lesser value

5. a. The range of $f(x) = 5 \cos \pi x$ on the given interval is $-5 \le f(x) \le 5$, so the minimum value of $f(x)$ on the interval is $-5$. From the graph, the minimum value of $g(x)$ on the interval is about $-6$, so $g(x)$ has the lesser minimum value.

   b. The maximum value of $f(x)$ on the interval is 5. From the graph, the maximum value of $g(x)$ on the interval is less than 3. So, $f(x)$ has a greater maximum value.

**Rubric**

a. 0.5 point for answer; 1 point for explanation

b. 0.5 point for answer; 1 point for explanation

6. a. The population of city A was 12,831 in 1900.

   The population of city B was 11,572 in 1900 ($t = 0$).

   City A had the greater population in 1900.

   b. The population of city A was increasing at 5% per year.

   The population of city B was increasing at 7% per year.

   The population of city B was increasing at the greater rate.

   c. For city A: $12,831(1.05)^{10} \approx 20,900$
   For city B: $11,572(1.07)^{10} \approx 22,764$
   City B had the greater population in 1910.

   d.

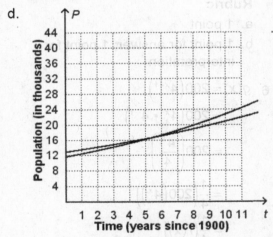

The populations were equal between $t = 5$ and $t = 6$, which was sometime in 1905.

**Rubric**

a. 0.5 point for each answer

b. 0.5 point for each answer

c. 0.5 point for each population; 1 point for city with greater population

d. 1 point

7. a. The amplitude of $d_1(t)$ is 4, so the displacement of mass $m_1$ varies between 4 centimeters and −4 centimeters relative to the equilibrium position of the mass (before the spring was compressed). This means that the spring attached to mass $m_1$ was compressed 4 centimeters initially. The table shows the displacement of mass $m_2$ varying between 6 centimeters and −6 centimeters relative to the equilibrium position of the mass (before the spring was compressed), so the amplitude of $d_2(t)$ is 6. This means that the spring attached to mass $m_2$ was compressed 6 centimeters initially. So, the spring attached to mass $m_2$ was compressed farther initially.

b. Mass $m_1$ is oscillating faster. The period of $d_1(t)$ is $\dfrac{2\pi}{\frac{\pi}{4}} = (2\pi)\left(\dfrac{4}{\pi}\right) =$ 8 seconds. The period of $d_2(t)$ is 16 seconds, because it takes the mass 16 seconds to return to its initial position.

## Rubric

a. 1 point for answer;
   2 points for explanation
b. 1 point for answer;
   2 points for explanation

# F.BF.1a* Answers

1. C

2. D

3. A

4. A, D, F

5. Let $\ell$, in inches, be the length of the rectangle. The perimeter of the rectangle is 200 inches.

$$2\ell + 2w = 200, \text{so } \ell = 100 - w.$$

$$A(w) = w(100 - w)$$
$$= 100w - w^2$$

**Rubric**

2 points

6.

$$C(b) = (575 + 375)b + \frac{1295}{7}$$
$$= 950b + 185$$

**Rubric**

2 points

7. $P(0) = 1000$ and $P(t + 1) = 2P(t)$ for $t \geq 0$

$P(t) = 1000(2)^t$

**Rubric**

1 point for each rule

8. a. $2\ell + 4w = 1800$, so $\ell = 900 - 2w$.

$$A(w) = \frac{w(900 - 2w)}{3}$$
$$= 300w - \frac{2}{3}w^2$$

b. The graph of $A(w)$ is a parabola that opens downward. The maximum value of $A(w)$ occurs at the vertex. Complete the square to write $A(w)$ in vertex form.

$$A(w) = 300w - \frac{2}{3}w^2$$
$$= -\frac{2}{3}(w^2 - 450w)$$
$$= -\frac{2}{3}(w^2 - 450w + 225^2) + 33,750$$
$$= -\frac{2}{3}(w - 225)^2 + 33,750$$

The maximum value of $A(w)$ is 33,750 square meters.

c. The domain of $A(w)$ is $0 < w < 450$ because the width must be positive ($w > 0$) and the length must be positive ($900 - 2w > 0$, or $w < 450$). The range of $A(w)$ is $0 < A(w) < 33,750$.

**Rubric**

a. 2 points

b. 2 points

c. 0.5 point for the domain; 0.5 point for the range

9. a. An annual interest rate of 3% is $\frac{3\%}{12} = 0.25\%$ per month.

1) Multiply the balance from the previous month by 0.0025 to determine the interest owed for the past month.

2) Add this interest to the balance from the previous month.

3) Subtract the monthly payment from this amount.

b. $B(0) = 100,000$ and $B(p + 1) = 1.0025B(p) - 690.58$ for $p \geq 0$

**Rubric**

a. 2 points

b. 2 points

# F.BF.1b* Answers

1. A

2. B, C, E

3. Let $w$ be the width of the pool, so the length of the pool is $3w$. Let $A_B(w)$ be the area of the bottom of the pool.

$$A_B(w) = 3w \cdot w = 3w^2$$

Let $A_W(w)$ be the combined area of the pair of sides of the pool along the width.

Note that 6 inches is $\frac{1}{2}$ foot.

$$A_w(w) = 2 \cdot w \cdot \frac{1}{2} = w$$

Let $A_L(w)$ be the combined area of the pair of sides of the pool along the length.

$$A_L(w) = 2 \cdot 3w \cdot \frac{1}{2} = 3w$$

To write a function for the total area $A(w)$ that needs to be tiled, find the sum of the areas of the bottom and sides of the pool.

$$A(w) = A_B(w) + A_W(w) + A_L(w)$$
$$= 3w^2 + 3w + w$$
$$= 3w^2 + 4w$$

Now multiply the area function by the cost per unit area to get the cost function $C(w)$.

$$C(w) = 3.75 \cdot A(w)$$
$$= 3.75(3w^2 + 4w)$$
$$= 11.25w^2 + 15w$$

The function $C(w) = 11.25w^2 + 15w$ relates the cost of the tile needed to the width of the pool.

**Rubric**

1 point for defining variables;
1 point for area function;
1 point for cost function

4. The fraction $F$ of the students at the high school from town B at time $t$ is the number of students from town B divided by the total number of students.

$$F(t) = \frac{N_B(t)}{N_A(t) + N_B(t) + N_C(t)}$$
$$= \frac{227(1.051)^t}{341(1.055)^t + 227(1.051)^t + 112(1.059)^t}$$

**Rubric**

2 points

5. Let $V_1(x)$ be the function that models the volume, in cubic inches, of the prism with edge lengths of $x + 1$ inches, $x + 2$ inches, and $x + 3$ inches.

$$V_1(x) = (x+1)(x+2)(x+3)$$
$$= x^3 + 6x^2 + 11x + 6$$

Let $V_2(x)$ be the function that models the volume, in cubic inches, of the prism with edge lengths of $x + 2$ inches, $x + 3$ inches, and $x + 4$ inches.

$$V_2(x) = (x+2)(x+3)(x+4)$$
$$= x^3 + 9x^2 + 26x + 24$$

Let $D(x)$ be the function that models the positive difference, in cubic inches, between the volumes of these prisms. Note that each edge length of the prism with volume $V_2(x)$ is 1 inch greater than the corresponding edge length of the prism with volume $V_1(x)$, so $V_2(x) > V_1(x)$ over the domain $x \geq 0$.

$$D(x) = V_2(x) - V_1(x)$$
$$= x^3 + 9x^2 + 26x + 24 -$$
$$(x^3 + 6x^2 + 11x + 6)$$
$$= 3x^2 + 15x + 18$$

**Rubric**

1 point for each correct function

6. Use the fact that the amount $A$, in dollars, of an investment as a function of time $t$, in years, is given by $A(t) = A_0\left(1 + \dfrac{r}{n}\right)^{nt}$, where $A_0$ is the initial amount, $r$ is the annual interest rate as a decimal, and $n$ is the number of compounding periods per year.

The amount in Marcelle's certificate of deposit is $A_{CD}(t) = 1250(1.0025)^{12t}$.

The amount in Marcelle's money market account is $A_{MM}(t) = 1000(1.015)^{4t}$.

The amount in Marcelle's retirement fund is $A_{RF}(t) = 5000(1.07)^t$.

So, the total amount in Marcelle's investments is

$A(t) = A_{CD}(t) + A_{MM}(t) + A_{RT}(t)$

$= 1250(1.0025)^{12t} + 1000(1.015)^{4t} + 500(1.07)^t$.

**Rubric**

2 points

7. a. $C(n) = 2n + 175$

b. $R(n) = 27n$

c. $P(n) = R(n) - C(n)$

$= 27n - (2n + 175)$

$= 25n - 175$

d. To determine the break-even point, set the profit function equal to 0 and solve for $n$.

$25n - 175 = 0$

$25n = 175$

$n = 7$

So, Yousef needs to sell 7 cases to break even.

**Rubric**

1 point for each part

8. a. Since the bar rotates counterclockwise, the wheel that contains the rider initially moves down, so use a function of the form $h_W(t) = -a \sin bt + k$ to model the height $h_W$, in feet, of the center of the wheel at time $t$, in seconds.

$a = \dfrac{50}{2} = 25$

$b = \dfrac{2\pi}{12} = \dfrac{\pi}{6}$

At time $t = 0$, the height of the center of the wheel is 45 feet, so $h_W(0) = 45$.

$h_W(t) = -25 \sin \dfrac{\pi}{6} t + k$

$h_W(0) = -25 \sin \dfrac{\pi}{6} \cdot 0 + k$

$45 = -25 \sin 0 + k$

$45 = k$

So, the function

$h_W(t) = -25 \sin \dfrac{\pi}{6} t + 45$ models the

height, in feet, of the center of the wheel that contains the rider $t$ seconds after the ride begins.

b. Since the wheel rotates counterclockwise, the rider initially moves down, so use a function of the form $h_R(t) = -a \sin bt + k$ to model the height $h_R$, in feet, of the rider relative to the center of the wheel at time $t$, in seconds.

$a = \dfrac{30}{2} = 15$

$b = \dfrac{2\pi}{5}$

At time $t = 0$, the height of the rider relative to the center of the wheel is 0 feet, so $h_R(0) = 0$.

$h_R(t) = -15 \sin \dfrac{2\pi}{5} t + k$

$h_R(0) = -15 \sin \dfrac{2\pi}{5} \cdot 0 + k$

$0 = -15 \sin 0 + k$

$0 = k$

So, the function $h_R(t) = -15 \sin \dfrac{2\pi}{5} t$

models the height, in feet, of the rider relative to the center of the wheel that contains the rider $t$ seconds after the ride begins.

c. The sum of the functions from parts a and b models the height $h$, in feet, of the rider relative to the ground $t$ seconds after the ride begins.

$$h(t) = h_R(t) + h_W(t)$$

$$= \left(-15 \ \sin \ \frac{2\pi}{5}t\right) +$$

$$\left(-25 \ \sin \ \frac{\pi}{6}t + 45\right)$$

$$= -15 \ \sin \ \frac{2\pi}{5}t - 25 \ \sin \ \frac{\pi}{6}t + 45$$

**Rubric**

2 points for each part

# F.BF.2* Answers

1. B

2. D

3. B, C, F

4. a. $t(1) = 40$, $t(d) = t(d - 1) + 5$, for $2 \le d \le 10$

   b. $t(d) = 5(d - 1) + 40$

   c. $t(8) = 5(8 - 1) + 40$
   $$= 5(7) + 40$$
   $$= 35 + 40$$
   $$= 75$$

   Calvin practices for 75 minutes on the 8th day.

   **Rubric**

   a. 1 point

   b. 1 point

   c. 0.5 point for answer; 0.5 point for showing work

5. a. This sequence is geometric because the ratios of consecutive terms are approximately equal.
   $$\frac{54.15}{57} = 0.95, \frac{51.44}{54.15} \approx 0.95,$$
   $$\frac{48.87}{51.44} \approx 0.95$$

   The common ratio is approximately 0.95.

   b. $s(t) = 57(0.95)^{t-1}$

   c. $s(1) = 57$, $s(t) = s(t - 1) \cdot 0.95$, for $t \ge 2$

   d. The speed of the car is 60 feet per second when it begins to coast.
   Substitute 0 for $t$ in the explicit formula, $s(t) = 57(0.95)^{t-1}$.
   $$s(0) = 57(0.95)^{0-1}$$
   $$= 57(0.95)^{-1}$$
   $$= 60$$

   **Rubric**

   1 point for each part

6. a. An arithmetic sequence models this situation because there is a common difference between every term.
   $$334 - 306 = 28$$
   $$362 - 334 = 28$$
   $$390 - 362 = 28$$

   b. Since the common difference is 28 and the first term of the sequence is $c(2) = 306$ when $p = 2$, an explicit formula that models this situation is $c(p) = 306 + 28(p - 2)$ for $p \ge 2$.
   A recursive formula that models this situation is $c(2) = 306$, $c(p) = c(p - 1) + 28$, for $p \ge 3$.

   c. Substitute 44 for $p$ in the explicit formula, $c(p) = 306 + 28(p - 2)$.
   $$c(p) = 306 + 28(44 - 2)$$
   $$= 306 + 28(42)$$
   $$= 306 + 1176$$
   $$= 1482$$

   It would cost \$1,482 for 44 people to attend the party.

   **Rubric**

   a. 1 point for answer; 1 point for justification

   b. 1 point for explicit formula; 1 point for recursive formula; 1 point for showing work

   c. 0.5 point for answer; 0.5 point for showing work

# F.BF.3 Answers

1. B

2. B, C, F

3. Possible answer: The graph of $f(x)$ is reflected across the $x$-axis, vertically shrunk by a factor of $\frac{1}{2}$, and shifted left 3 units and down 3 units to obtain the graph of $g(x)$.

$$g(x) = -\frac{1}{2}(x+3)^3 - 3$$

(Note: Other equivalent forms of this function are possible if students identified transformations different from the ones given.)

**Rubric**
2 points for transformations;
1 point for rule

4. Possible answer: The graph of $f(x)$ is reflected across the $y$-axis, shifted left 4 units, reflected across the $x$-axis, and shifted up 2 units to obtain the graph of $g(x)$.

$$g(x) = -3^{-(x+4)} + 2$$

(Note: Other equivalent forms of this function are possible if students identified transformations different from the ones given.)

**Rubric**
2 points for transformations;
1 point for rule

5. Carlos's interpretation of the horizontal shift is incorrect. Since 2 is being subtracted from $x$ in the argument of the logarithm, the graph of the parent function will shift right 2 units.

Carlos's interpretation of the vertical stretch is correct. However, he did not notice that the coefficient of the logarithm is negative, and so the graph of the parent function will be reflected across the $x$-axis.

Carlos's interpretation of the vertical shift is incorrect. Since 3 is being added to the function, the graph of the parent function will shift up 3 units.

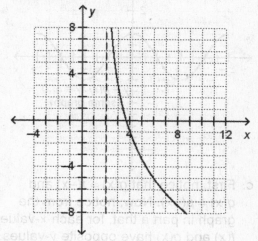

**Rubric**
1 point for stating Carlos's statement of the stretch factor is correct;
1 point for recognizing Carlos forgot the reflection;
1 point for recognizing the error in Carlos's horizontal shift statement;
0.5 point for correcting it;
1 point for recognizing the error in Carlos's vertical shift statement;
0.5 point for correcting it;
2 points for the correct graph

6. a The graph of $g(x)$ is a reflection across the $y$-axis of the graph of $f(x)$.

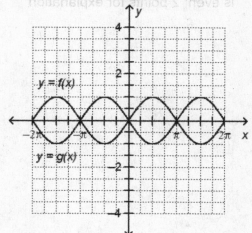

b. The graph of $q(x)$ is a reflection across the $y$-axis of the graph of $p(x)$.

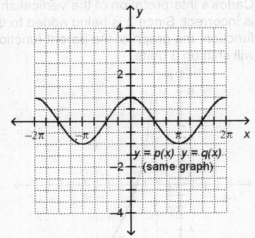

$y = p(x)$; $y = q(x)$
(same graph)

c. First, notice that $g(x) = f(-x)$ and $q(x) = p(-x)$. Now, notice from the graph in part a that, for each $x$-value, $f(x)$ and $g(x)$ have opposite $y$-values. So, $g(x) = -f(x)$. Since $g(x) = f(-x)$ as well, you can conclude that $f(-x) = -f(x)$, which means that the parent sine function is odd. Now, notice from the graph in part b that, for each $x$-value, $p(x) = q(x)$. Since $q(x) = p(-x)$ as well, you can conclude that $p(x) = p(-x)$, which means that the parent cosine function is even.

**Rubric**

a. 1 point for each graph
b. 1 point for each graph
c. 1 point for stating $f(x)$ is odd and $p(x)$ is even; 2 points for explanation

# F.BF.4a Answers

1. B

2. C

3. B, D

4.

$$f(x) = \frac{1}{2}\sqrt[3]{x+4} - 5$$

$$y = \frac{1}{2}\sqrt[3]{x+4} - 5$$

$$y + 5 = \frac{1}{2}\sqrt[3]{x+4}$$

$$2(y+5) = \sqrt[3]{x+4}$$

$$2y + 10 = \sqrt[3]{x+4}$$

$$(2y+10)^3 = x+4$$

$$(2y+10)^3 - 4 = x$$

So, the inverse of $f(x)$ is

$f^{-1}(x) = (2x+10)^3 - 4$.

**Rubric**

1 point for inverse;
1 point for accurate work

5.

$$f(x) = \sqrt{x-2}$$

$$y = \sqrt{x-2}$$

$$y^2 = x - 2$$

$$y^2 + 2 = x$$

So, the inverse of $f(x)$ is $f^{-1}(x) = x^2 + 2$.

The domain of $f^{-1}(x)$ should be the same as the range of $f(x)$. Similarly, the range of $f^{-1}(x)$ should be the same as the domain of $f(x)$. The domain of $f(x)$ is $x \geq 2$, and the range of $f(x)$ is $f(x) \geq 0$. So, the domain of $f^{-1}(x)$ is $x \geq 0$, and the range is $f^{-1}(x) \geq 2$.

**Rubric**

1 point for inverse; 1 point for accurate work; 2 points for domain and range

6. a. The domain of $f(x)$ is all real numbers $x$ such that $x \neq 9$. The range of $f(x)$ is all real numbers $y$ such that $y \neq 4$.

b.

$$f(x) = \frac{4x+3}{x-9}$$

$$y = \frac{4x+3}{x-9}$$

$$y(x-9) = 4x+3$$

$$yx - 9y = 4x+3$$

$$yx - 4x = 9y+3$$

$$x(y-4) = 9y+3$$

$$x = \frac{9y+3}{y-4}$$

So, the inverse of $f(x)$ is

$f^{-1}(x) = \frac{9x+3}{x-4}$.

c. The domain of $f^{-1}(x)$ is the same as the range of $f(x)$: all real numbers $x$ such that $x \neq 4$. The range of $f^{-1}(x)$ is the same as the domain of $f(x)$: all real numbers $y$ such that $y \neq 9$.

**Rubric**

1 point for each part

7.

$$f(x) = 15(4)^{x-2} + 7$$

$$y = 15(4)^{x-2} + 7$$

$$y - 7 = 15(4)^{x-2}$$

$$\frac{y-7}{15} = 4^{x-2}$$

$$\log_4 \frac{y-7}{15} = \log_4 4^{x-2}$$

$$\log_4 \frac{y-7}{15} = (x-2)\log_4 4$$

$$\log_4 \frac{y-7}{15} = x - 2$$

$$\log_4 \left(\frac{y-7}{15}\right) + 2 = x$$

So, the inverse of $f(x)$ is

$f^{-1}(x) = \log_4\left(\frac{x-7}{15}\right) + 2$.

To find $x$ such that $f(x) = 247$, find $f^{-1}(247)$.

$$f^{-1}(247) = \log_4\left(\frac{247-7}{15}\right) + 2$$
$$= \log_4 16 + 2$$
$$= \log_4 4^2 + 2$$
$$= 2\log_4 4 + 2$$
$$= 4$$

So, $f(x) = 247$ when $x = 4$.

### Rubric
1 point for inverse;
1 point for accurate work;
1 point for using inverse to find $x$;
1 point for accurate work

8. The function that expresses $t$ as a function of $p$ is the inverse of $p(t)$. In this situation, do not switch $t$ and $p$ so as to avoid confusing the meaning of $p$ and $t$ in terms of the context. Just replace $p(t)$ with $p$ and solve for $t$ in terms of $p$.

$$p(t) = 1000(2)^t$$
$$p = 1000(2)^t$$
$$\frac{p}{1000} = 2^t$$
$$\log_2 \frac{p}{1000} = \log_2 2^t$$
$$\log_2 \frac{p}{1000} = t\log_2 2$$
$$\log_2 \frac{p}{1000} = t$$

So, the function $t(p) = \log_2 \frac{p}{1000}$ models the time $t$, in weeks after the initial population was observed, as a function of the current population $p$.

$$t(32,000) = \log_2 \frac{32,000}{1000}$$
$$= \log_2 32$$
$$= \log_2 2^5$$
$$= 5\log_2 2$$
$$= 5$$

So, it will take 5 weeks for the population to grow to 32,000. Verify this value of $t$ by finding $p(5)$.

$$p(5) = 1000(2)^5$$
$$= 1000(32)$$
$$= 32,000$$

### Rubric
1 point for $t(p)$, the inverse of $p(t)$;
1 point for accurate work finding $t(p)$;
1 point for finding $t(32,000)$; 1 point for accurate work finding $t(32,000)$; 1 point for finding $p(5)$

9. a. $p(d) = \sqrt{d^3}$
$$p = \sqrt{d^3}$$
$$p^2 = d^3$$
$$\sqrt[3]{p^2} = d$$

So, the inverse of $p(d)$ is $d(p) = \sqrt[3]{p^2}$.

b. The inverse function models the distance between a planet and the Sun as a function of the planet's orbital period.

c. $d(11.86) = \sqrt[3]{11.86^2} \approx$ 5.2 astronomical units

### Rubric
a. 1 point for the inverse function;
   1 point for accurate work
b. 1 point
c. 1 point for the inverse function;
   1 point for accurate work

# F.LE.4* Answers

1. D

2. A

3. B, C, E

4. Set $N(t)$ equal to 1,000,000 and solve for $t$.

$$1{,}000{,}000 = 500(2)^{0.5t}$$

$$2000 = (2)^{0.5t}$$

$$\log 2000 = \log (2)^{0.5t}$$

$$3 + \log 2 = 0.5t \log 2$$

$$\frac{3 + \log 2}{0.5 \log 2} = t$$

$$\frac{6}{\log 2} + 2 = t$$

$$22 \approx t$$

So, the population will reach 1,000,000 after $\dfrac{6}{\log 2} + 2$ hours, which is about 22 hours.

**Rubric**

1 point for writing and solving the equation; 1 point for the correct exact solution; 1 point for the correct approximate solution

5. Substitute 0.00005 for $[H^+]$ and solve for pH.

$$10^{-pH} = [H^+]$$

$$10^{-pH} = 0.00005$$

$$\log 10^{-pH} = \log 0.00005$$

$$-pH \log 10 = \log (5 \times 10^{-5})$$

$$-pH = \log 5 - 5$$

$$pH = -\log 5 + 5$$

$$pH \approx 4.3$$

So, the pH of the substance is about 4.3.

**Rubric**

1 point for writing and solving the equation; 1 point for the correct answer

6. Set $T(t)$ equal to 125 and solve for $t$.

$$125 = 72 + 140e^{-0.14t}$$

$$\frac{53}{140} = e^{-0.14t}$$

$$\ln \frac{53}{140} = \ln e^{-0.14t}$$

$$\ln \frac{53}{140} = -0.14t$$

$$\frac{\ln \frac{53}{140}}{-0.14} = t$$

$$7 \approx t$$

So, the tea will be cool enough to serve after sitting for 7 minutes.

**Rubric**

1 point for writing and solving the equation; 1 point for the correct answer

7. The error is incorrectly applying the properties of logarithms by writing log 5375 − log 7 as log (5375 − 7) = log 5368, because log 5375 − log 7 ≠ log (5375 − 7).

Correct solution:

$$7(10)^{0.25x} = 5375$$

$$10^{0.25x} = \frac{5375}{7}$$

$$\log 10^{0.25x} = \log \frac{5375}{7}$$

$$0.25x \log 10 = \log \frac{5375}{7}$$

$$0.25x = \log \frac{5375}{7}$$

$$x = 4 \log \frac{5375}{7}$$

$$x \approx 11.54$$

**Rubric**

1 point for identifying the error; 1 point for the correct solution

8. a. Let $B$, in dollars, be the account balance as a function of the time $t$, in years. The function $B(t) = 500e^{0.03t}$ models the account balance. Set $B(t)$ equal to 1500 and solve for $t$.

$$1500 = 500e^{0.03t}$$
$$3 = e^{0.03t}$$
$$\ln 3 = \ln e^{0.03t}$$
$$\ln 3 = 0.03t$$
$$\frac{\ln 3}{0.03} = t$$
$$36.6 \approx t$$

So, the account balance would triple after $\dfrac{\ln 3}{0.03}$ years, which is about 36.6 years.

b. Let $r$ be the annual interest rate as a decimal. The function $B(r) = 500e^{20r}$ models the account balance as a function of $r$. Set $B(r)$ equal to 1500 and solve for $r$.

$$1500 = 500e^{20r}$$
$$3 = e^{20r}$$
$$\ln 3 = \ln e^{20r}$$
$$\ln 3 = 20r$$
$$\frac{\ln 3}{20} = r$$
$$0.055 \approx r$$

The amount in the account would triple after 20 years if the annual interest rate were $\dfrac{\ln 3}{20}$, which is about 5.5%.

**Rubric**

a. 1 point for developing the correct equation; 1 point for a correct exact solution; 1 point for the correct approximate solution

b. 1 point for developing the correct equation; 1 point for a correct exact solution; 1 point for the correct approximate solution

9. The function $L(t) = 844 \cdot 2^{-\frac{t}{3.8}}$ models the radioactivity level in the room.

Set $L(t)$ equal to 4 and solve for $t$.

$$4 = 844 \cdot 2^{-\frac{t}{3.8}}$$
$$\frac{1}{211} = 2^{-\frac{t}{3.8}}$$
$$\log_2 \frac{1}{211} = \log_2 2^{-\frac{t}{3.8}}$$
$$\log_2 \frac{1}{211} = -\frac{t}{3.8}$$
$$-3.8 \log_2 \frac{1}{211} = t$$
$$30 \approx t$$

So, the radioactivity level will be below 4 picoCuries per liter after 30 days.

**Rubric**
1 point for writing the correct function; 2 points for writing and solving the equation; 1 point for the correct number of days

# F.LE.5* Answers

1. C

2. A

3. D

4. A, D, H

5. A large plain cheese pizza has 0 additional toppings. Since $C(0) = 8.5$, a large cheese pizza from this restaurant costs $8.50.

**Rubric**

2 points

6. The formula for the amount $A$ in an account with initial amount $A_0$ that earns interest compounded continuously at an annual rate $r$, as a decimal, after $t$ years is $A = A_0 e^{rt}$. In $A(t) = 500e^{0.03t}$, the value that corresponds to $r$ is 0.03, which is 3%. So, the account earns 3% annual interest.

**Rubric**

2 points

7. The general function $A(t) = A_0(1 + R)^t$ models the amount $A$ in an account with an initial amount of $A_0$ and an effective annual rate of $R$, as a decimal, after $t$ years. Write the function for each bank in this form.

$$A_1(t) = 425(1.00625)^{4t}$$
$$= 425(1.00625^4)^t$$
$$\approx 425(1.02524)^t$$

The effective annual rate for an account at bank 1 is about 2.524%.

$$A_2(t) = 425(1.00175)^{12t}$$
$$= 425(1.00175^{12})^t$$
$$\approx 425(1.02120)^t$$

The effective annual rate for an account at bank 2 is about 2.120%.

So, bank 1 offers the account with the higher effective annual rate.

**Rubric**

1 point for each effective annual rate; 1 point for identifying the bank with the higher effective annual rate

8. a. Evaluate $A(t) = 750(0.7937)^t$ at $t = 0$ to find the initial amount of fermium-253 in the sample.

$$A(0) = 750(0.7937)^0$$
$$= 750(1)$$
$$= 750$$

So, the initial amount of fermium-253 in the sample is 750 grams.

b. The value 0.7937 indicates that each day after the first, there is 79.37% of the fermium-253 compared to the day before.

c. In $A(t) = 750(0.7937)^t$, the percent of fermium-253 remaining after each day is 79.37%. To find the half-life, you want to know how long it takes for the percent to be 50%. Solve the equation $(0.7937)^t = 0.5$.

$$(0.7937)^t = 0.5$$
$$\ln (0.7937)^t = \ln 0.5$$
$$t \ln 0.7937 = \ln 0.5$$
$$t = \frac{\ln 0.5}{\ln 0.7937}$$
$$t \approx 3$$

So, the half-life of fermium-253 is about 3 days.

**Rubric**

a. 1 point for correct amount; 1 point for reasonable explanation

b. 1 point for a reasonable interpretation

c. 1 point for correct half-life; 1 point for reasonable explanation

9. a. The coefficient of $t$ is the rate of change of the car's position relative to the next rest area. You can confirm this by directly calculating the rate of change:

$$\text{rate of change} = \frac{d(1) - d(0)}{1 - 0}$$

$$= \frac{35 - 100}{1} = -65$$

Since the rate of change is $-65$, the car is approaching the next rest area at 65 miles per hour.

b. At $t = 0$, the car is just passing the first rest stop. So, the distance to the second rest stop is $d(0) = 100$ miles.

### Rubric

a. 1 point for correct speed with correct units; 1 point for a reasonable explanation

b. 1 point for correct distance with correct units; 1 point for a reasonable explanation

# F.TF.1 Answers

1. B
2. C
3. C
4. A, C, F, G
5. The radian measure of a central angle in a circle is defined to be the length of the arc that the angle intercepts measured in terms of the circle's radius. For instance, if a central angle intercepts an arc of length 3 units on a circle with radius 3 units, then the arc contains $\frac{3}{3} = 1$ "radius unit." So, the radian measure of the angle is 1. Similarly, if a central angle intercepts an arc of length 6 units on a circle with radius 3 units, then the arc contains $\frac{6}{3} = 2$ "radius units." So, the radian measure of the angle is 2. In general, if a central angle in a circle of radius $r$ intercepts an arc of length $s$, then the angle's radian measure is $\theta = \frac{s}{r}$. On the unit circle, the radius is 1. So, $\theta = \frac{s}{1} = s$. In other words, the radian measure $\theta$ is equal to the arc length $s$ on the unit circle.

**Rubric**
2 points

6. If a central angle in a circle of radius $r$ intercepts an arc of length $s$, then the angle's radian measure is $\theta = \frac{s}{r}$. So, for the given radius and arc length,
$\theta = \frac{10\pi}{8} = \frac{5\pi}{4}$.
If a central angle in the unit circle intercepts an arc of length $s$, then the angle's radian measure is $\theta = s$. In this case, $\theta$ is known. So, $\frac{5\pi}{4} = s$. The length of the arc intercepted by a central angle of $\frac{5\pi}{4}$ radians is $\frac{5\pi}{4}$ units.

**Rubric**
1 point for answer;
1 point for explanation

7. Consider what happens to the endpoint that is not fixed at (1, 0) when the length of the arc is doubled, tripled, and so on. Doubling the arc length puts the endpoint in Quadrant II. Tripling puts the endpoint in Quadrant II near the x-axis. Quadrupling puts the endpoint in Quadrant III. Quintupling puts the endpoint in Quadrant IV. Sextupling puts the endpoint in Quadrant IV near the x-axis.

   a. The arc's endpoint is in Quadrant IV but not near the x-axis, so the measure of $\alpha$ is 5 radians.

   b. The arc's endpoint is in Quadrant II near the x-axis, so the measure of $\beta$ is 3 radians.

**Rubric**
1 point for each part

8. If a central angle in the unit circle intercepts an arc of length $s$, then the angle's radian measure is $\theta = s$. So, the measure of the central angle that intercepts the given arc is $\frac{11\pi}{6}$ radians.

The arc length formula can be used to find the arc lengths on the other circles. The arc length formula is $s = r\theta$, where $s$ is the arc length, $r$ is the radius of the circle, and $\theta$ is the central angle of the arc.

The length $s$ on the circle of radius 2 units is $s = 2\left(\frac{11\pi}{6}\right) = \frac{11\pi}{3}$ units.

The length $s$ on the circle of radius 3 units is $s = 3\left(\frac{11\pi}{6}\right) = \frac{11\pi}{2}$ units.

The length $s$ on the circle of radius 4 units is $s = 4\left(\frac{11\pi}{6}\right) = \frac{22\pi}{3}$ units.

**Rubric**
1 point for recognizing the measure of the central angle;
1 point for each arc length on the other circles;
1 point for reasonable justifications and work

9. If a central angle in a circle of radius $r$ intercepts an arc of length $s$, then the angle's radian measure is $\theta = \frac{s}{r}$. Use this formula to find the measure of angle $\alpha$.

$$\alpha = \frac{15\pi}{10} = \frac{3\pi}{2}\text{ radians}$$

The measure of $\theta$ on the unit circle is half of $\alpha$. So, the measure of $\theta$ is $\frac{1}{2} \cdot \frac{3\pi}{2} = \frac{3\pi}{4}$ radians.

If a central angle in the unit circle intercepts an arc of length $s$, then the angle's radian measure is $\theta = s$. In this case, $\theta$ is known. So, $\frac{3\pi}{4} = s$. The length of the arc intercepted by a central angle of $\frac{3\pi}{4}$ on the unit circle is $\frac{3\pi}{4}$ units.

So, Dean and Sasha should use Sasha's answer.

**Rubric**
1 point for finding $\alpha$;
1 point for finding $\theta$;
1 point for a reasonable explanation;
1 point for the answer

80

# F.TF.2 Answers

1. B

2. D

3. A, D, E

4. a. The angle of rotation $\pi$ in standard position traverses an arc on the unit circle. The rotation ends at the point $(-1, 0)$, and the $y$-coordinate of this point is the value of $\sin \pi$.
So, $\sin \pi = 0$.

   b. The angle of rotation $\dfrac{4\pi}{3}$ in standard position traverses an arc on the unit circle. The rotation ends at the point $\left(-\dfrac{1}{2}, -\dfrac{\sqrt{3}}{2}\right)$, and the $x$-coordinate of this point is the value of $\cos\dfrac{4\pi}{3}$.
So, $\cos\dfrac{4\pi}{3} = -\dfrac{1}{2}$.

   c. The angle of rotation $\dfrac{2\pi}{3}$ in standard position traverses an arc on the unit circle. The rotation ends at the point $\left(-\dfrac{1}{2}, \dfrac{\sqrt{3}}{2}\right)$, and the ratio of the $y$-coordinate of this point to the $x$-coordinate of this point is the value of $\tan\dfrac{2\pi}{3}$.
So, $\tan\dfrac{2\pi}{3} = \dfrac{\dfrac{\sqrt{3}}{2}}{-\dfrac{1}{2}} = \dfrac{\sqrt{3}}{2}(-2) = -\sqrt{3}$.

**Rubric**
a. 0.5 point for each part
b. 0.5 point for each part
c. 0.5 point for each part

5. a. Possible answer: The angle of rotation $\dfrac{14\pi}{3}$ in standard position traverses the unit circle more than once. To find a coterminal angle between 0 and $2\pi$, subtract the appropriate multiple of $2\pi$ from the angle of rotation. Notice that $\dfrac{14\pi}{3} - 2(2\pi) = \dfrac{2\pi}{3}$. The angle of rotation $\dfrac{2\pi}{3}$ in standard position traverses an arc on the unit circle. The rotation ends at the point $\left(-\dfrac{1}{2}, \dfrac{\sqrt{3}}{2}\right)$, and the $y$-coordinate of this point is the value of $\sin\dfrac{2\pi}{3}$.
So, $\sin\dfrac{14\pi}{3} = \sin\dfrac{2\pi}{3} = \dfrac{\sqrt{3}}{2}$.

   b. Possible answer: The angle of rotation $\dfrac{59\pi}{6}$ in standard position traverses the unit circle more than once. To find a coterminal angle between 0 and $2\pi$, subtract the appropriate multiple of $2\pi$ from the angle of rotation. Notice that $\dfrac{59\pi}{6} - 4(2\pi) = \dfrac{11\pi}{6}$. The angle of rotation $\dfrac{11\pi}{6}$ in standard position traverses an arc on the unit circle. The rotation ends at the point $\left(\dfrac{\sqrt{3}}{2}, -\dfrac{1}{2}\right)$, and the $x$-coordinate of this point is the value of $\cos\dfrac{11\pi}{6}$.
So, $\cos\dfrac{59\pi}{6} = \cos\dfrac{11\pi}{6} = \dfrac{\sqrt{3}}{2}$.

**Rubric**
a. 1 point for description of how to find the trigonometric function value; 0.5 point for finding it

b. 1 point for description of how to find the trigonometric function value; 0.5 point for finding it

6. a. Possible answer: The angle of rotation $-\dfrac{19\pi}{3}$ in standard position traverses the unit circle in a clockwise direction more than once. To find a coterminal angle between 0 and $2\pi$, add the appropriate multiple of $2\pi$ to the angle of rotation. Notice that $-\dfrac{19\pi}{3} + 4(2\pi) = \dfrac{5\pi}{3}$. The angle of rotation $\dfrac{5\pi}{3}$ in standard position traverses an arc on the unit circle. The rotation ends at the point $\left(\dfrac{1}{2}, -\dfrac{\sqrt{3}}{2}\right)$, and the ratio of the y-coordinate of this point to the x-coordinate of this point is the value of $\tan\dfrac{5\pi}{3}$.

So,
$$\tan\left(-\dfrac{19\pi}{3}\right) = \tan\dfrac{5\pi}{3}$$
$$= \dfrac{-\dfrac{\sqrt{3}}{2}}{\dfrac{1}{2}}$$
$$= -\dfrac{\sqrt{3}}{2}(2) = -\sqrt{3}.$$

b. Possible answer: The angle of rotation $-\dfrac{3\pi}{4}$ in standard position traverses the unit circle in a clockwise direction. To find a coterminal angle between 0 and $2\pi$, add the appropriate multiple of $2\pi$ to the angle of rotation. Notice that $-\dfrac{3\pi}{4} + 2\pi = \dfrac{5\pi}{4}$. The angle of rotation $\dfrac{5\pi}{4}$ in standard position traverses an arc on the unit circle. The rotation ends at the point $\left(-\dfrac{\sqrt{2}}{2}, -\dfrac{\sqrt{2}}{2}\right)$, and the y-coordinate of this point is the value of $\sin\dfrac{5\pi}{4}$.

So, $\sin\left(-\dfrac{3\pi}{4}\right) = \sin\dfrac{5\pi}{4} = -\dfrac{\sqrt{2}}{2}$.

**Rubric**
a. 1 point for description of how to find the trigonometric function value; 0.5 point for finding it
b. 1 point for description of how to find the trigonometric function value; 0.5 point for finding it

7. a. The length of the arc from A to B is 1 unit. The y-coordinate of point B is about 0.8 or 0.9. So, $\sin 1 \approx 0.8$ or $\sin 1 \approx 0.9$ (either is acceptable).

b. The length of the arc from A to G is 6 units. The x-coordinate of point G is about 0.9 or 1. So, $\cos 6 \approx 0.9$ or $\cos 6 \approx 1$ (either is acceptable).

c. The length of the arc from A to C is 2 units. The x-coordinate of point C is about −0.4, and the y-coordinate is about 0.9. So, $\tan 2 \approx \dfrac{0.9}{-0.4} \approx -2.3$.

d. The lengths of the arcs from $A$ to $F$ and from $A$ to $G$ are 5 and 6 units, respectively. The length of the arc from $A$ to halfway between $F$ and $G$ is 5.5 units. The coordinates of this point are about $(0.7, -0.7)$.

So, $\tan 5.5 \approx \dfrac{-0.7}{0.7} = -1.0$.

**Rubric**

a. 1 point

b. 1 point

c. 1 point

d. 2 points

8. A complete revolution of the unit circle is $2\pi$, not $\pi$, so the student should have repeatedly subtracted $2\pi$ from $\theta$ until the result is between 0 and $2\pi$.

$$\cos \frac{19\pi}{6} = \cos \frac{7\pi}{6} = -\frac{\sqrt{3}}{2}$$

**Rubric**

2 points for explanation; 1 point for correct value

9. For $\theta$ between 0 and $2\pi$, the angle traverses an arc on the unit circle before completing one full revolution. The arc ends at a point $(x, y)$. The $y$-coordinate of the endpoint of the arc is the value of $\sin \theta$. The $x$-coordinate of the endpoint of the arc is the value of $\cos \theta$. The ratio of the $y$-coordinate to the $x$-coordinate of the endpoint of the arc is the value of $\tan \theta$. So, for $0 \le \theta \le 2\pi$, $\sin \theta = y$, $\cos \theta = x$,

and $\tan \theta = \dfrac{y}{x}$.

For $\theta < 0$ or $\theta > 2\pi$, find a coterminal angle between 0 and $2\pi$ as follows.

- For $\theta < 0$, add a complete revolution of the unit circle, $2\pi$, to $\theta$ as many times as needed until a value between 0 and $2\pi$ is obtained.

- For $\theta > 2\pi$, subtract a complete revolution of the unit circle, $2\pi$, from $\theta$ as many times as needed until a value between 0 and $2\pi$ is obtained.

The coterminal angle has the same trigonometric values as the original angle.

**Rubric**

1 point each for the unit circle definitions of the trigonometric functions;

1 point for recognizing that values of $\theta$ outside the range $0 \le \theta \le 2\pi$ are treated differently;

1 point for explaining the process of using the unit circle to find trigonometric values with $\theta < 0$;

1 point for explaining the process of using the unit circle to find trigonometric values with $\theta > 2\pi$

# F.TF.5* Answers

1. D
2. B
3. E
4. G
5. B
6. C
7. D
8. F
9. B, C, F

10. a. The passenger enters the Ferris wheel at a height of 15 meters at time $t = 0$. The height at the top of the Ferris wheel is $15 + 2(75) = 165$ meters, and the Ferris wheel completes 1 revolution every 30 minutes. From this information, it can be expected that the passenger will be at a height of 15 meters at $t = 0$ minutes, a height of 90 meters at $t = 7.5$ minutes, a height of 165 meters at $t = 15$ minutes, and a height of 90 meters at $t = 22.5$ minutes. These values are all given by both Mike's model and Lupe's model.

$h_1(0) = 75 \sin \dfrac{\pi}{15}(0 - 7.5) + 90$

$\qquad = 75 \sin \left(-\dfrac{\pi}{2}\right) + 90$

$\qquad = 75(-1) + 90 = 15$

$h_1(7.5) = 75 \sin \dfrac{\pi}{15}(7.5 - 7.5) + 90$

$\qquad = 75 \sin 0 + 90$

$\qquad = 75(0) + 90 = 90$

$h_1(15) = 75 \sin \dfrac{\pi}{15}(15 - 7.5) + 90$

$\qquad = 75 \sin \dfrac{\pi}{2} + 90$

$\qquad = 75(1) + 90 = 165$

$h_1(22.5) = 75 \sin \dfrac{\pi}{15}(22.5 - 7.5) + 90$

$\qquad = 75 \sin \pi + 90$

$\qquad = 75(0) + 90 = 90$

$h_2(0) = 75 \cos \dfrac{\pi}{15}(0 - 15) + 90$

$\qquad = 75 \cos (-\pi) + 90$

$\qquad = 75(-1) + 90 = 15$

$h_2(7.5) = 75 \cos \dfrac{\pi}{15}(7.5 - 15) + 90$

$\qquad = 75 \cos \left(-\dfrac{\pi}{2}\right) + 90$

$\qquad = 75(0) + 90 = 90$

$h_2(15) = 75 \cos \dfrac{\pi}{15}(15 - 15) + 90$

$\qquad = 75 \cos 0 + 90$

$\qquad = 75(1) + 90 = 165$

$h_2(22.5) = 75 \cos \dfrac{\pi}{15}(22.5 - 15) + 90$

$\qquad = 75 \cos \dfrac{\pi}{2} + 90$

$\qquad = 75(0) + 90 = 90$

b. Periodic phenomena can be modeled by either a sine function or a cosine function. Applying the appropriate horizontal shift to one function will produce the other.

**Rubric**

a. 2 points

b. 2 points

11. Since the top of the piston is at the lowest position at time $t = 0$, use a function of the form $h(t) = -a \cos bt + k$.

The amplitude is $a = \dfrac{9.3 - 0}{2} = 4.65$ cm.

The frequency is

$750 \cdot \dfrac{1}{60} = 12.5$ revolutions per second,

so $b = 12.5 \cdot 2\pi = 25\pi$.

The minimum displacement of the piston is 0 centimeters, and the maximum displacement is 9.3 centimeters. The midline is halfway between the minimum and maximum displacements of the piston. Find the average of these two values and vertically shift the graph up that many units.

$$k = \frac{9.3 + 0}{2} = 4.65$$

So, $h(t) = -4.65 \cos 25\pi t + 4.65$.

**Rubric**

1 point for choosing cosine since the piston starts at its lowest position;
1 point for $a$;
1 point for $b$;
1 point for $k$

(Note: While a student should choose cosine based on the initial position of the piston, partial credit should be awarded if the student correctly finds a sine model.)

12. a. A cosine function of the form $a(t) = \cos bt$ can be used to model the appearance of a target on a disc. For each disc, choose a value of $b$ such that the cosine function takes on its maximum value each time one of the disc's 4 targets appears.

For the disc on the left that rotates once every 2 seconds, it takes 2 seconds for each of the 4 targets to reach the highest position on the disc, so 1 target reaches the highest position every $\frac{1}{2}$ second, which means that $b = \frac{2\pi}{\frac{1}{2}} = 4\pi$. So, the $t$-values for which the function $a_L(t) = \cos 4\pi t$ attains its maximum value models the times when targets are visible.

For the disc in the middle that rotates once every 3 seconds, it takes 3 seconds for each of the 4 targets to reach the highest position on the disc, so 1 target reaches the highest position every $\frac{3}{4}$ second, which means that $b = \frac{2\pi}{\frac{3}{4}} = \frac{8\pi}{3}$. So, the $t$-values for which the function $a_M(t) = \cos \frac{8\pi t}{3}$ attains its maximum value models the times when targets are visible.

For the disc on the right that rotates once every 4 seconds, it takes 4 seconds for each of the 4 targets to reach the highest position on the disc, so 1 target reaches the highest position every 1 second, which means that $b = \frac{2\pi}{1} = 2\pi$. So, the $t$-values for which the function $a_R(t) = \cos 2\pi t$ attains its maximum value models the times when targets are visible.

b. If the player shoots at time $t = 7.8$, the pistol is ready to shoot again at time $t = 7.8 + 0.1 + 0.3 = 8.2$. If the player shoots immediately, then the time at which the water hits the target is $t = 8.2 + 0.2 = 8.4$. Examine the functions at time $t = 8.4$.

$$a_L(8.4) = \cos 4\pi(8.4) = \cos 33.6\pi$$

$$a_M(8.4) = \cos \frac{8\pi(8.4)}{3} = \cos \frac{67.2\pi}{3}$$

$$a_R(8.4) = \cos 2\pi(8.4) = \cos 16.8\pi$$

Then, determine the $t$-value for which the argument of each function will become the closest multiple of $2\pi$ that is greater than the current argument of the function.

$$a_L(t) = \cos 34\pi \text{ when } t = \frac{34\pi}{4\pi} = 8.5.$$

$$a_M(t) = \cos 24\pi \text{ when } t = \frac{24\pi}{\frac{8\pi}{3}} = 9.$$

$$a_R(t) = \cos 18\pi \text{ when } t = \frac{18\pi}{2\pi} = 9.$$

So, the function that will next attain its maximum value is $a_L(t)$. This means that the next target the player can try to hit is on the left disc. Since the pulse of water reaches the left disc at time $t = 8.4$ but the target isn't visible until time $t = 8.5$, the player should wait 0.1 second after the pistol is ready to fire again. This is 0.7 second after the last time the player pulled the trigger.

### Rubric
a. 1 point for each correct model
b. 1 point for correct target; 1 point for a correct time

# F.TF.8 Answers

1. A

2. A

3. D

4. C, D, G, H

5. a. The unit circle definitions of sine, cosine, and tangent are $\sin \theta = y$, $\cos \theta = x$, and $\tan \theta = \dfrac{y}{x}$, where $\theta$ is an angle of rotation in standard position whose terminal side crosses the unit circle at the point $(x, y)$. Substitute $\sin \theta$ for $y$ and $\cos \theta$ for $x$ in the definition for $\tan \theta$.

$$\tan \theta = \frac{\sin \theta}{\cos \theta}$$

b. Solve $\tan \theta = \dfrac{\sin \theta}{\cos \theta}$ for $\sin \theta$.

$$\tan \theta = \frac{\sin \theta}{\cos \theta}$$
$$\tan \theta \cos \theta = \sin \theta$$

c. Solve $\tan \theta = \dfrac{\sin \theta}{\cos \theta}$ for $\cos \theta$.

$$\tan \theta = \frac{\sin \theta}{\cos \theta}$$
$$\tan \theta \cos \theta = \sin \theta$$
$$\cos \theta = \frac{\sin \theta}{\tan \theta}$$

**Rubric**

a. 1 point for identity;
   1 point for explanation

b. 1 point for identity

c. 1 point for identity

6. Since $\dfrac{\pi}{2} < \theta < \pi$, $\sin \theta$ is positive and $\tan \theta$ is negative.

$$\sin^2 \theta + \cos^2 \theta = 1$$
$$\sin^2 \theta + (-0.7702)^2 = 1$$
$$\sin^2 \theta = 1 - (-0.7702)^2$$
$$\sin \theta = \pm\sqrt{1 - (-0.7702)^2}$$
$$\sin \theta \approx \pm 0.6378$$

Since $\sin \theta$ is positive for $\dfrac{\pi}{2} < \theta < \pi$,

$\sin \theta \approx 0.6378$.

$$\tan \theta = \frac{\sin \theta}{\cos \theta}$$
$$\approx \frac{0.6378}{-0.7702}$$
$$\approx -0.8281$$

So, $\tan \theta \approx -0.8281$.

**Rubric**

0.5 point each for the signs of $\sin \theta$ and $\tan \theta$; 1 point for $\sin \theta$; 1 point for $\tan \theta$

7. Simon did not take into account that the square root of $\cos^2 \theta$ can be positive or negative. The sign of $\cos \theta$ is dependent upon the quadrant in which the terminal side of $\theta$ falls. Since $\pi < \theta < \dfrac{3\pi}{2}$, the terminal side of $\theta$ is in Quadrant III. So, both $\sin \theta$ and $\cos \theta$ will be negative. Correct work is shown below, starting from where Simon made his mistake.

$$\cos^2 \theta \approx 0.085988$$
$$\cos \theta \approx \pm\sqrt{0.085988}$$
$$\cos \theta \approx \pm 0.293237$$

Since $\pi < \theta < \dfrac{3\pi}{2}$, the terminal side of $\theta$ is in Quadrant III, where $\cos \theta$ is negative. So, $\cos \theta \approx -0.2932$.

$$\sin \theta \approx (3.2603)(-0.293237) \approx -0.9560$$

**Rubric**

1 point for recognizing the sign error;
1 point each for the correct values of $\sin \theta$ and $\cos \theta$

8. The equation of the unit circle is $x^2 + y^2 = 1$. For an angle of rotation $\theta$ in standard position whose terminal side crosses the unit circle at the point $(x, y)$, the unit circle definitions of sine and cosine are $\sin \theta = y$ and $\cos \theta = x$. Substitute $\sin \theta$ for $y$ and $\cos \theta$ for $x$ and apply the commutative property.

$$x^2 + y^2 = 1$$
$$\cos^2 \theta + \sin^2 \theta = 1$$
$$\sin^2 \theta + \cos^2 \theta = 1$$

So, $\sin^2 \theta + \cos^2 \theta = 1$.

**Rubric**

3 points

9. a. For an angle of rotation $\theta$ in standard position whose terminal side crosses the unit circle at the point $(x, y)$, the unit circle definition of tangent is

$\tan \theta = \dfrac{y}{x}$. Since $\tan \theta$ is positive, $x$ and $y$ have the same sign, which happens in Quadrants I and III. So, the terminal side of $\theta$ lies in Quadrant I or Quadrant III.

b. Use the identity $\cos \theta = \dfrac{\sin \theta}{\tan \theta}$ and the Pythagorean identity $\sin^2 \theta + \cos^2 \theta = 1$.

$$\cos \theta = \frac{\sin \theta}{\tan \theta}$$
$$= \frac{\sin \theta}{0.6966}$$

Substitute $\dfrac{\sin \theta}{0.6966}$ for $\cos \theta$ in the Pythagorean identity and solve for $\sin \theta$.

$$\sin^2 \theta + \cos^2 \theta = 1$$
$$\sin^2 \theta + \left(\frac{\sin \theta}{0.6966}\right)^2 = 1$$
$$\sin^2 \theta + \left(\frac{1}{0.6966}\right)^2 \sin^2 \theta = 1$$
$$\sin^2 \theta + 2.0608 \sin^2 \theta \approx 1$$
$$3.0608 \sin^2 \theta \approx 1$$
$$\sin^2 \theta \approx 0.3267$$
$$\sin \theta \approx \pm\sqrt{0.3267}$$
$$\sin \theta \approx \pm 0.5716$$

So, $\sin \theta \approx 0.5716$ for $\theta$ in Quadrant I, and $\sin \theta \approx -0.5716$ for $\theta$ in Quadrant III.

c. Find $\cos \theta$ when $\sin \theta \approx 0.5716$ and $\theta$ is in Quadrant I.
$$\sin^2 \theta + \cos^2 \theta = 1$$
$$(0.5716)^2 + \cos^2 \theta = 1$$
$$\cos^2 \theta = 1 - (0.5716)^2$$
$$\cos \theta = \pm\sqrt{1 - (0.5716)^2}$$
$$\cos \theta \approx \pm 0.8205$$

Since $\theta$ is in Quadrant I, $\cos \theta \approx 0.8205$.

Now find $\cos \theta$ when $\sin \theta \approx -0.5716$ and $\theta$ is in Quadrant III.
$$\sin^2 \theta + \cos^2 \theta = 1$$
$$(-0.5716)^2 + \cos^2 \theta = 1$$
$$\cos^2 \theta = 1 - (-0.5716)^2$$
$$\cos \theta = \pm\sqrt{1 - (-0.5716)^2}$$
$$\cos \theta \approx \pm 0.8205$$

Since $\theta$ is in Quadrant III, $\cos \theta \approx -0.8205$.

(Answers may vary slightly due to the method the student uses to find each of the values.)

**Rubric**

a. 0.5 point for each correct quadrant; 1 point for explanation

b. 0.5 point for each value of $\sin \theta$; 1 point for reasonable work

c. 0.5 point for each value of $\cos \theta$; 1 point for reasonable work

# G.GPE.2 Answers

1. B

2. A

3. D

4. A, D, F

5. Let $P(x, y)$ be any point on the parabola. The point $Q(x, 3)$ is the point on the directrix that is closest to $P$. By the distance formula, $FP = \sqrt{x^2 + (y+3)^2}$ and $QP = \sqrt{(x-x)^2 + (y-3)^2} = |y-3|$. By the definition of a parabola, $FP = QP$.

$$\sqrt{x^2 + (y+3)^2} = |y-3|$$

$$x^2 + (y+3)^2 = |y-3|^2$$

$$x^2 + y^2 + 6y + 9 = y^2 - 6y + 9$$

$$x^2 = -12y$$

$$-\frac{1}{12}x^2 = y$$

## Rubric

1 point for answer; 2 points for appropriate work using the distance formula

6. a. $y = -\frac{1}{8}x^2$

b.

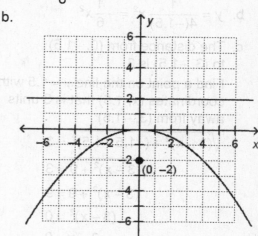

c. The segment from the focus (0, –2) to the point (0, 2) has length 4. The midpoint of the segment is the origin, (0, 0). Therefore, the vertex is the origin.

## Rubric

a. 1 point

b. 1 point for parabola; 0.5 point for focus; 0.5 point for directrix

c. 1 point for answer; 1 point for explanation

7. Eric incorrectly expanded $(y - 7)^2$ as $y^2 + 49$. The correct expansion is $(y - 7)^2 = y^2 - 14y + 49$. The rest of the work is shown below.

$$x^2 + (y - 7)^2 = |y + 7|^2$$

$$x^2 + y^2 - 14y + 49 = y^2 + 14y + 49$$

$$x^2 = 28y$$

$$\frac{1}{28}x^2 = y$$

The correct equation is $y = \frac{1}{28}x^2$.

## Rubric

1 point for finding the mistake; 1 point for correct expansion; 1 point for correct work to complete the problem; 1 point for the equation

8. a. The focus $(0, p)$ is $(0, -1.5)$, so $p = -1.5$. The directrix is $y = -p = -(-1.5) = 1.5$.

   b. $y = \dfrac{1}{4(-1.5)} x^2 = -\dfrac{1}{6} x^2$

   c. The distance from $(0, -1.5)$ to $(3, -1.5)$ is 3.

   Find a point on the line $y = 1.5$ with coordinates $(x, 1.5)$ that is 3 units away from $(3, -1.5)$.

   $$\sqrt{(3-x)^2 + (-1.5-1.5)^2} = 3$$
   $$\sqrt{(3-x)^2 + 9} = 3$$
   $$(3-x)^2 + 9 = 9$$
   $$(3-x)^2 = 0$$
   $$3 - x = 0$$
   $$x = 3$$

   The point $(3, 1.5)$ is on $y = 1.5$ and 3 units away from $(3, -1.5)$.

   a. 1 point
   b. 1 point
   c. 1 point for the distance from $(0, -1.5)$ to $(3, -1.5)$; 1 point for finding $(3, 1.5)$.

9. a. $(x, -p)$
   b. $QP$
   c. $|y + p|$
   d. $y^2 + 2py + p^2$; $2py$; $4py$; $\dfrac{1}{4p} x^2$

**Rubric**
   a. 1 point
   b. 1 point
   c. 1 point (for generality, the answer must include absolute value notation)
   d. 0.5 point for each answer

# S.ID.4* Answers

1. C
2. B
3. A, C
4. C
5. H
6. E
7. G
8. A
9. D

10. a. $z_{80} = \dfrac{80 - 100}{15} = -\dfrac{20}{15} \approx -1.3$;

   $P(z \le z_{80}) \approx 0.0968 = 9.68\%$

   b. $z_{127} = \dfrac{127 - 100}{15} = \dfrac{27}{15} = 1.8$;

   $P(z \le z_{127}) \approx 0.9641 = 96.41\%$

**Rubric**
1 point for each part

11. a. $z_{35} = \dfrac{35 - 45.5}{3.92} = -\dfrac{10.5}{3.92} \approx -2.7$;

   $P(z > z_{35}) = 1 - P(z \le z_{35}) \approx 0.9965 = 99.65\%$

   b. $z_{50} = \dfrac{50 - 45.5}{3.92} = \dfrac{4.5}{3.92} \approx 1.1$;

   $P(z > z_{50}) = 1 - P(z \le z_{35}) \approx 0.1357 = 13.57\%$

**Rubric**
1 point for each part

12. His error is that 451 grams represents only 1 standard deviation below the mean, not 2 standard deviations below the mean.

To correct his error, subtract the percent of the population that falls between 2 standard deviations below the mean and 1 standard deviation below the mean.

$95 - \dfrac{95 - 68}{2} = 95 - 13.5$

$= 81.5$

So, about 81.5% of the grapefruits have masses between 451 grams and 544 grams.

**Rubric**
1 point for identifying the error; 2 points for the correct estimate

13. a. Since the heights of the male students in Bart's class are normally distributed, 50% of the students will be taller than the mean height. So, 50% of the male students in Bart's class are more than 68 inches tall.

   b. Since $64 = 68 - 2(2)$, the value is 2 standard deviations below the mean. The 68-95-99.7 rule indicates that 95% will be within 2 standard deviations, 4 inches, of the mean height. Male students less than 64 inches tall are half of the 5% of male students who are taller than $68 + 4 = 72$ inches or shorter than $68 - 4 = 64$ inches. So, 2.5% of the male students in Bart's class are less than 64 inches tall.

**Rubric**
a. 1 point for answer;
   1 point for explanation

b. 1 point for answer;
   1 point for recognizing the given height is 2 standard deviations from the mean;
   1 point for recognizing that it's necessary to divide the 5% by 2

14. a. $z_{70} = \dfrac{70 - 82}{5} = -\dfrac{12}{5} = -2.4$ and

$z_{75} = \dfrac{75 - 82}{5} = -\dfrac{7}{5} = -1.4;$

$P(z_{70} \le z \le z_{75}) =$

$P(z \le z_{75}) - P(z \le z_{70}) =$

$0.0808 - 0.0082 = 0.0726 = 7.26\%$

So, 7.26% of the students scored between 70 and 75 on the test.

b. $z_{90} = \dfrac{90 - 82}{5} = \dfrac{8}{5} = 1.6;$

$P(z \ge z_{90}) = 1 - P(z \le z_{90}) =$

$1 - 0.9452 = 0.0548 = 5.48\%$

So, 5.48% of the students scored at least 90 on the test.

c. $z_{65} = \dfrac{65 - 82}{5} = -\dfrac{17}{5} = -3.4;$

$P(z \le z_{65}) = 0.0003 = 0.03\%$

So, 0.03% of the students scored at most 65 on the test.

**Rubric**

a. 1 point for percent; 1 point for work

b. 1 point for percent; 1 point for work

c. 1 point for percent; 1 point for work

# S.IC.1* Answers

1. A
2. C
3. B
4. A, D, F
5. Since a random sample is more likely to produce a representative sample, Veata should use the values from the group to which she was randomly assigned. The best estimate for the percentage of students at the school who are left-hand dominant is $\frac{1}{8} = 12.5\%$.

   **Rubric**
   1 point for identifying the correct sample;
   1 point for a reasonable explanation;
   1 point for the correct estimate

6. Yes, since a random sample is likely to produce a representative sample, the rancher can infer that the mean weight of the population, all of the calves, is about the same as the mean weight of the sample.

   **Rubric**
   1 point for correct answer; 2 points for a reasonable explanation

7. From the poll of 500 registered voters, the proportion of registered voters who support the candidate is $\frac{271}{500} = 0.542$, which is greater than 50%. From the poll of 300 registered voters, the proportion of registered voters who support the candidate is $\frac{144}{300} = 0.48$, which is less than 50%. Since both polls used random samples, either is a good estimate of the proportion of the registered voters that support the candidate. Since increasing the sample size tends to decrease the variability in the sample, the poll that surveyed 500 registered voters provides the better estimate. So, the candidate should expect to meet more registered voters who support her.

**Rubric**
1 point for correct answer; 2 points for a reasonable explanation

8. Arturo's sample is a convenience sample, which is unlikely to be representative. Since all of the observations are for one location at one time of day, the sample is representative of the cars that pass that location at that time of day, but not of all the cars that pass through the neighborhood.

Bernice's sample is a stratified sample, which can be representative. Since the location and time of each observation are random, the sample is likely to be representative of all the cars that pass through the neighborhood.

Since Chu only observes cars he believes are speeding, his sample is biased. A biased sample cannot be representative of all the cars that pass through the neighborhood.

The best estimate of the average speed is the result from the sample that is most likely to be representative of the population, which is the mean for Bernice's sample, 30 mph.

**Rubric**
1 point for each evaluation; 1 point for identifying the best estimate

# S.IC.2* Answers

1. A

2. C

3. B, C, D, F

4. Yes. The probability of rolling a 2 four times in a row using a fair number cube is

$$\left(\frac{1}{6}\right)^4 \approx 0.0008 = 0.08\%,$$ which is very

unlikely. So, it is unlikely the number cube is fair.

**Rubric**
1 point for stating the number cube is unlikely fair; 2 points for a reasonable explanation

5. The results are very unlikely for the given model. Since C has the greatest probability of occurring and A has the least, you would expect C to have a greater number of outcomes than A, not the opposite. Another way to look at it is this: Since $P(C) = P(A) + P(B)$, you would expect the number of outcomes for C to be approximately equal to the total number of outcomes for A and B, but this is not the case.

**Rubric**
1 point for stating the results are unlikely; 2 points for a reasonable explanation

6. a. There are 16 possible outcomes: 1 has a sum of 2, 2 have a sum of 3, 3 have a sum of 4, 4 have a sum of 5, 3 have a sum of 6, 2 have a sum of 7, and 1 has a sum of 8. Since the outcomes are equally likely, divide each number of outcomes associated with a particular sum by 16.

| Sum | Probability |
|-----|-------------|
| 2 | $\frac{1}{16}$ |
| 3 | $\frac{2}{16} = \frac{1}{8}$ |
| 4 | $\frac{3}{16}$ |
| 5 | $\frac{4}{16} = \frac{1}{4}$ |
| 6 | $\frac{3}{16}$ |
| 7 | $\frac{2}{16} = \frac{1}{8}$ |
| 8 | $\frac{1}{16}$ |

b.

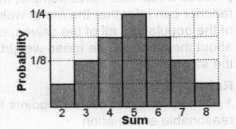

c. The shape of the probability distribution is reasonably close to the shape of Ronaldo's dot plot, so the model is consistent with the results. The differences can be attributed to random variation rather than a problem with the model.

**Rubric**
a. 2 points for completing the table correctly
b. 1 point for a correct histogram
c. 1 point for correct answer; 1 point for a reasonable explanation

7. The probability of rolling a 4 is $\frac{1}{6}$, so the probability of not rolling a 4 is $1 - \frac{1}{6} = \frac{5}{6}$.

The probability of not rolling a 4 $n$ times is $\left(\frac{5}{6}\right)^n$.

| $n$ | $P$(not a 4) |
|---|---|
| 5 | $\left(\frac{5}{6}\right)^5 \approx 0.402 = 40.2\%$ |
| 10 | $\left(\frac{5}{6}\right)^{10} \approx 0.162 = 16.2\%$ |
| 15 | $\left(\frac{5}{6}\right)^{15} \approx 0.065 = 6.5\%$ |
| 20 | $\left(\frac{5}{6}\right)^{20} \approx 0.026 = 2.6\%$ |
| 25 | $\left(\frac{5}{6}\right)^{25} \approx 0.010 = 1.0\%$ |

Not rolling a 4 in 20 or 25 rolls is very unlikely, so Jean could conclude the number cube is not fair after either of these numbers of rolls. (Actually, the probability of not rolling a 4 after 17 rolls of a fair number cube is less than 5%, so Jean could conclude the number cube is not fair any time after 17 rolls.)

## Rubric
2 points for making a correct table of probabilities;
1 point for stating a reasonable number of rolls;
1 point for a reasonable explanation

8. $P$(1 four times in a row) = $(P(1))^4 =$ $(0.2)^4 = 0.0016 = 0.16\%$

$P$(2 four times in a row) = $(P(2))^4 =$ $(0.5)^4 = 0.0625 = 6.25\%$

$P$(3 four times in a row) = $(P(3))^4 =$ $(0.3)^4 = 0.0081 = 0.81\%$

While all of these outcomes are unlikely, the probability that the spinner lands on 1 four times in a row and the probability that the spinner lands on 3 four times in a row are both less than 1%, which should cause you to question the model.

## Rubric
1 point for each probability;
1 point for describing which results call the model into question;
1 point for a reasonable explanation

# S.IC.3* Answers

1. C
2. D
3. A
4. A, D, E
5. Surveys measure characteristics of interest. Observational studies determine whether existing conditions (factors) are related to characteristics of interest. Experiments determine whether imposed conditions (treatments) have cause-and-effect relationships with characteristics of interest.

   **Rubric**
   1 point for each description

6. Study A is an experiment and study B is an observational study because the researchers in study A impose which teaching method is followed, whereas in study B the researchers observe the results of the existing teaching methods.

   **Rubric**
   2 points

7. Randomization in surveys and observational studies is limited to randomly selecting the subjects. Such randomization increases the likelihood the samples are representative of the populations.

   Randomization is included in experiments by randomly assigning subjects to either a treatment group or a control group. Such randomization reduces the influence of any confounding variables on the characteristics of interest, which allows experiments to establish cause-and-effect relationships.

   **Rubric**
   3 points

8. a. The characteristic of interest is the number of eggs hens lay.
   b. This research study is an experiment because the researchers create different conditions.
   c. The treatment is the hours of light per day.
   d. Possible answer:
      The researchers could randomly assign the hens to the coops. Such randomization could reduce the influence of other factors, such as age and breed, that affect the number of eggs hens lay.
   e. Yes, an experiment can establish a cause-and-effect relationship. If the number of eggs laid by the hens in one coop is significantly different than the number of eggs laid by the hens in the other coop, then the difference in egg production can be attributed to the difference in the amount of light per day that the hens received.

   **Rubric**
   1 point for each part

9. a. The characteristic of interest is the incidence of lung cancer.
   b. This research study is an observational study because the researchers are investigating whether an existing condition is related to a characteristic of interest. The researchers do not impose a condition on the subjects.
   c. The factor is exposure to asbestos.
   d. Possible answer:
      The researchers could randomly select the subjects for the study from the populations of people exposed to asbestos and people never exposed to asbestos. Such randomization could reduce the influence of other factors, such as smoking, that affect the incidence lung cancer.

e. No, an observational study can only establish that a relationship exists, not cause and effect. Even if the study shows that the incidence of lung cancer is significantly greater in people who were exposed to asbestos, it's possible that other factors, such as smoking, played the determining role. Perhaps the asbestos exposure amplified the negative effects of smoking, or perhaps there simply were more smokers among the people exposed to asbestos. In either case, smoking (and not asbestos exposure) could be the actual cause of lung cancer.

**Rubric**
1 point for each part

# S.IC.4* Answers

1. B

2. A

3. A, B, D, F

4. $\hat{p} = \dfrac{417}{1000} = 0.417$

$$0.417 - 2\sqrt{\dfrac{0.417(1-0.417)}{1000}} \le p \le 0.417 + 2\sqrt{\dfrac{0.417(1-0.417)}{1000}}$$

$$0.386 \le p \le 0.448$$

The estimate is that between 38.6% and 44.8% of the registered voters in the state plan to vote for the proposition.

**Rubric**

1 point for correct sample proportion; 1 point for correct interval

5. $\hat{p} = \dfrac{4}{25} = 0.16$

$$0.16 - 1.96\sqrt{\dfrac{0.16(1-0.16)}{25}} \le p \le 0.16 + 1.96\sqrt{\dfrac{0.16(1-0.16)}{25}}$$

$$0.016 \le p \le 0.304$$

**Rubric**

1 point for correct sample proportion; 1 point for correct interval

6. a. The interval from $0.6 - 0.07 = 0.53$ to $0.6 + 0.07 = 0.67$ contains $8 + 9 + 11 + 13 + 11 + 10 + 9 = 71$ of the 100 sample proportions, so a confidence interval of 71% corresponds to a margin of error of ±7%.

   b. Since 90 of the 100 sample proportions are contained in the interval from $0.6 - 0.11 = 0.49$ to $0.6 + 0.11 = 0.71$, the margin of error for a 90% confidence interval is ±11%.

**Rubric**

2 points

7.

$$57.2 - 2.576\left(\dfrac{1.5}{\sqrt{200}}\right) \le \mu \le 57.2 + 2.576\left(\dfrac{1.5}{\sqrt{200}}\right)$$

$$56.9 \le \mu \le 57.5$$

A 99% confidence interval for the mean mass of the eggs for this breed is between 56.9 grams and 57.5 grams.

**Rubric**

1 point for correct margin of error; 1 point for correct interval

8. First find a 95% confidence interval for the proportion of students with severe peanut allergies, rounding to five decimal places.

$$\frac{2}{200} - 1.96\sqrt{\frac{\frac{2}{200}\left(1-\frac{2}{200}\right)}{200}} \le p \le \frac{2}{200} + 1.96\sqrt{\frac{\frac{2}{200}\left(1-\frac{2}{200}\right)}{200}}$$

$$-0.00379 \le p \le 0.02379$$

Since a negative proportion is not possible, a 95% confidence interval for the population proportion is 0 to 0.02379. Now multiply the number of students in the district by the maximum proportion to determine the maximum number of students the district serves who have severe peanut allergies.

$19,000 \cdot 0.02379 \approx 452$

The district serves an estimated maximum of 452 students who have severe peanut allergies.

### Rubric

2 points for correct interval; 1 point for estimate of maximum

9. a. Since $1 - 0.53 = 0.47$, the margins of error for the confidence intervals for both candidates are the same, $\sqrt{\dfrac{0.53 \cdot 0.47}{300}} \approx 0.0288$.

The estimate for the proportion of voters in the district who support the candidate:

$$0.53 - 1.96(0.0288) \le p \le 0.53 + 1.96(0.0288)$$
$$0.474 \le p \le 0.586$$

The estimate for the proportion of voters in the district who support the opponent:

$$0.47 - 1.96(0.0288) \le p \le 0.47 + 1.96(0.0288)$$
$$0.414 \le p \le 0.526$$

b. The estimates for the proportion of voters in the district supporting each candidate show that it is not unlikely that, for example, 52% of the voters support the opponent and only 48% support the candidate, so the candidate would not be wise to take a break.

### Rubric

a. 1 point for correct margin of error;
0.5 point for each correct interval

b. 1 point for stating the candidate should not take a break;
1 point for using the interval to explain

# S.IC.5* Answers

1. C

2. D

3. The mean distance with the new type of bat is 340.5 feet.

   The mean distance with the standard bat is 324.5 feet.

   Since 340.5 − 324.5 = 16 feet, which is greater than 10.5 feet, there is evidence the player can hit balls farther using the new type of bat.

   **Rubric**

   3 points

4. The mean number of crabgrass plants per plot is 3 for the treated plots and 6.8 for the untreated plots. The difference of the means is 3 − 6.8 = −3.8.

   Since only 2 of the 100 differences in the resampling distribution are this small, the probability of randomly getting a difference this small is 0.02, so the result of the experiment is significant.

   Since the mean number of crabgrass plants is significantly lower in the plots treated with the new product, the experiment provides evidence that the new product prevents crabgrass from invading lawns.

   **Rubric**

   1 point for calculating the difference of the sample means;
   2 points for determining the probability of the difference;
   2 points for the conclusion

# S.IC.6* Answers

1. A

2. C

3. A, B, C, D, E, F

4. a. If the proportion of subjects with high blood cholesterol levels who develop heart disease is significantly greater than the proportion of subjects with normal blood cholesterol levels who develop heart disease, the results would support a claim that high blood cholesterol level is related to heart disease.

   b. Since this is an observational study, there are no results that would support a claim that high blood cholesterol causes heart disease.

   **Rubric**
   2 points for each part

5. Since this is an observational study, the researchers can claim that there is a relationship between using vibrating hand tools and vibration syndrome, but not that using vibrating hand tools causes vibration syndrome.

   **Rubric**
   3 points

6. Since this study is a randomized comparative experiment, it can establish a cause-and-effect relationship. The researchers can claim that the new drug reduces blood cholesterol levels.

   **Rubric**
   3 points

7. a. If the number of subjects who take the new drug and contract malaria is significantly less than the number of subjects who take the drug currently used to prevent malaria and contract malaria as well as the number of subjects in the control group who contract malaria, then the results would support a claim that the new drug is more effective.

   b. If the number of subjects who take the new drug and contract malaria is significantly more than the number of subjects who take the drug currently used to prevent malaria and contract malaria but significantly less than the number of subjects in the control group who contract malaria, then the results would support a claim that the new drug is less effective than the drug currently used to prevent malaria, but more effective than no drug.

   c. Possible answer:
   The health workers could fail to give the appropriate pill to each subject because the pills look alike.

   **Rubric**
   2 points for each part

# S.CP.1* Answers

1. B

2. A

3. G

4. C

5. B

6. B

7. Sample space:
{(H, H, 1), (H, T, 1), (T, H, 1), (T, T, 1),
(H, H, 2), (H, T, 2), (T, H, 2), (T, T, 2),
(H, H, 3), (H, T, 3), (T, H, 3), (T, T, 3),
(H, H, 4), (H, T, 4), (T, H, 4), (T, T, 4),
(H, H, 5), (H, T, 5), (T, H, 5), (T, T, 5),
(H, H, 6), (H, T, 6), (T, H, 6), (T, T, 6)}

Subset:
{(H, T, 1), (T, H, 1), (H, T, 4), (T, H, 4),
(H, T, 6), (T, H, 6)}

**Rubric**
2 points for sample space;
1 point for subset

8. a. The intersection of $A$ and $B$ $(A \cap B)$

b. Possible answer:
The union of $A$ and $C$ $(A \cup C)$ or the complement of $B$ $(B^c)$

c. The intersection of the complement of $A$ and the complement of $C$ $(A^c \cap C^c)$

d. The first scenario is impossible, because there are no marbles that are both red and yellow. The second and third scenarios are possible because the bag contains red marbles, blue marbles, and yellow marbles, which are not red or blue.

**Rubric**
a. 1 point
b. 1 point
c. 1 point
d. 1 point for explaining why a is impossible; 1 point for explaining why b and c are possible

9. a. $A = \{(1, 1), (2, 2), (3, 3), (4, 4), (5, 5), (6, 6), (7, 7), (8, 8), (9, 9), (10, 10)\}$

b. $B = \{(2, 2), (2, 3), (2, 5), (2, 7), (3, 2), (3, 3), (3, 5), (3, 7), (5, 2), (5, 3), (5, 5), (5, 7), (7, 2), (7, 3), (7, 5), (7, 7)\}$

c. $C$ is the intersection of $A$ and $B$.
$C = A \cap B = \{(2, 2), (3, 3), (5, 5), (7, 7)\}$

**Rubric**
a. 1 point
b. 2 points
c. 1 point for stating that $C$ is the intersection of $A$ and $B$; 1 point for elements

10. a. $A = \{3G, 1G, 2G, 4G\}$

b. $B = \{2Y, 2R, 2G, 2B\}$

c. $C = A \cap B = \{2G\}$

d. The subset is the intersection of the subset describing the spinner landing on the chosen color and the subset describing the spinner landing on the chosen number.

e. The spinner landing on a red section with the number 3:
$\{1R, 2R, 4R, 1R\} \cap \{3G, 3B, 3Y, 3Y\} = \varnothing$

The spinner landing on a yellow section with the number 1:
$\{2Y, 4Y, 3Y, 3Y\} \cap \{1R, 1G, 1B, 1R\} = \varnothing$

**Rubric**
a. 1 point
b. 1 point
c. 1 point
d. 1 point
e. 0.5 point for each set

# S.CP.2* Answers

1. a. No
   b. Yes
   c. Yes
   d. Yes

2. A, D

3. B

4. Yes, the events are independent.

   The sample space for rolling a fair number cube twice is
   $\{(1, 1), (1, 2), (1, 3), (1, 4), (1, 5), (1, 6), (2, 1), (2, 2), (2, 3), (2, 4), (2, 5), (2, 6), (3, 1), (3, 2), (3, 3), (3, 4), (3, 5), (3, 6), (4, 1), (4, 2), (4, 3), (4, 4), (4, 5), (4, 6), (5, 1), (5, 2), (5, 3), (5, 4), (5, 5), (5, 6), (6, 1), (6, 2), (6, 3), (6, 4), (6, 5), (6, 6)\}$.

   Outcomes where the first number is an even number are (2, 1), (2, 2), (2, 3), (2, 4), (2, 5), (2, 6), (4, 1), (4, 2), (4, 3), (4, 4), (4, 5), (4, 6), (6, 1), (6, 2), (6, 3), (6, 4), (6, 5), and (6, 6).

   Outcomes where the second number is 6 are (1, 6), (2, 6), (3, 6), (4, 6), (5, 6), and (6, 6).

   Outcomes where the first number is even and the second number is 6 are (2, 6), (4, 6), and (6, 6).

   $P(\text{first number is even}) = \dfrac{18}{36} = \dfrac{1}{2}$

   $P(\text{second number is 6}) = \dfrac{6}{36} = \dfrac{1}{6}$

   $P(\text{even and 6}) = \dfrac{3}{36} = \dfrac{1}{12}$

   $\dfrac{1}{12} = \dfrac{1}{2} \cdot \dfrac{1}{6}$, so the events are independent.

   **Rubric**
   1 point for answer;
   3 points for explanation

5. Picking a blue marble and picking a marble that has stripes are independent events.

   |  | Blue | Not blue | Total |
   |---|---|---|---|
   | **Striped** | 5 | 10 | 15 |
   | **Not striped** | 5 | 10 | 15 |
   | **Total** | 10 | 20 | 30 |

   $P(\text{blue}) = \dfrac{5+5}{30} = \dfrac{10}{30} = \dfrac{1}{3}$

   $P(\text{striped}) = \dfrac{5+10}{30} = \dfrac{15}{30} = \dfrac{1}{2}$

   $P(\text{blue and striped}) = \dfrac{5}{30} = \dfrac{1}{6} = \dfrac{1}{3} \cdot \dfrac{1}{2} =$
   $P(\text{blue}) \cdot P(\text{striped})$

   **Rubric**
   1 point for saying the events are independent; 2 points for explanation involving the product of the probabilities

6. $P(\text{male}) = \dfrac{12+5}{12+5+11+6} = \dfrac{17}{34} = \dfrac{1}{2}$

   $P(\text{adult}) = \dfrac{12+11}{34} = \dfrac{23}{34}$

   $P(\text{male and adult}) = \dfrac{12}{34} = \dfrac{6}{17}$

   $P(\text{male}) \cdot P(\text{adult}) = \dfrac{1}{2} \cdot \dfrac{23}{34} = \dfrac{23}{68}$

   Because $\dfrac{6}{17} \neq \dfrac{23}{68}$, $P(\text{male and adult}) \neq P(\text{male}) \cdot P(\text{adult})$, so the events are not independent.

   **Rubric**
   1 point for answer;
   2 points for explanation

7. $P(\text{white}) = \dfrac{120}{200} = \dfrac{3}{5}$

$P(\text{male}) = \dfrac{50}{200} = \dfrac{1}{4}$

Since the events are independent,
$P(\text{white and male}) = P(\text{white}) \cdot P(\text{male}) =$
$\dfrac{3}{5} \cdot \dfrac{1}{4} = \dfrac{3}{20}$.

Since $\dfrac{3}{20}$ of the population is white and
male and the population is 200, there are
$\dfrac{3}{20} \cdot 200 = 30$ mice that are white
and male.

**Rubric**

1 point for answer; 2 points for work

8. a. {(H, H), (H, T), (T, H), (T, T)}

b. When flipping a coin, the probability of
landing on heads is $\dfrac{1}{2}$.

From part a, there are four equally
likely outcomes when two coins are
flipped, so the probability of each is $\dfrac{1}{4}$.

$\dfrac{1}{2} \cdot \dfrac{1}{2} = \dfrac{1}{4}$, so the two events are
independent.

c. The sample space for flipping a coin
three times is {(H, H, H), (H, H, T),
(H, T, H), (T, H, H), (H, T, T),
(T, H, T), (T, T, H), (T, T, T)}.
The probability of each of these

outcomes is $\dfrac{1}{8}$.

$\dfrac{1}{2} \cdot \dfrac{1}{2} \cdot \dfrac{1}{2} = \dfrac{1}{8}$, so the three events
are independent.

**Rubric**

a. 1 point

b. 1 point for answer;
1 point for explanation

c. 1 point for answer;
1 point for explanation

9. a. $P(\text{right}) = \dfrac{130}{150} = \dfrac{13}{15}$

$P(\text{art}) = \dfrac{60}{150} = \dfrac{2}{5}$

$P(\text{right and art}) = \dfrac{52}{150} = \dfrac{26}{75}$

$P(\text{right}) \cdot P(\text{art}) = \dfrac{13}{15} \cdot \dfrac{2}{5} = \dfrac{26}{75} =$
$P(\text{right and art})$, so the events are
independent.

b. $P(\text{left}) = \dfrac{20}{150} = \dfrac{2}{15}$

$P(\text{left and art}) = \dfrac{8}{150} = \dfrac{4}{75}$

$P(\text{left}) \cdot P(\text{art}) = \dfrac{2}{15} \cdot \dfrac{2}{5} = \dfrac{4}{75} =$
$P(\text{left and art})$, so the events are
independent.

c. $P(\text{gym}) = \dfrac{90}{150} = \dfrac{3}{5}$

$P(\text{right and gym}) = \dfrac{78}{150} = \dfrac{13}{25}$

$P(\text{right}) \cdot P(\text{gym}) = \dfrac{13}{15} \cdot \dfrac{3}{5} = \dfrac{13}{25} =$
$P(\text{right and gym})$, so the events are
independent.

d. $P(\text{left and gym}) = \dfrac{12}{150} = \dfrac{2}{25}$

$P(\text{left}) \cdot P(\text{gym}) = \dfrac{2}{15} \cdot \dfrac{3}{5} = \dfrac{2}{25} =$
$P(\text{left and gym})$, so the events are
independent.

**Rubric**

a. 0.5 point for answer;
0.5 point for explanation

b. 0.5 point for answer;
0.5 point for explanation

c. 0.5 point for answer;
0.5 point for explanation

d. 0.5 point for answer;
0.5 point for explanation

# S.CP.3* Answers

1. C

2. D

3. A, B, F

4. There are 2 black threes in the deck, so

$$P(\text{black and three}) = \frac{2}{52} = \frac{1}{26}.$$

There are 26 black cards in the deck, so

$$P(\text{black}) = \frac{26}{52} = \frac{1}{2}.$$

$$P(\text{three} \mid \text{black}) = \frac{P(\text{black and three})}{P(\text{black})} =$$

$$\frac{\frac{1}{26}}{\frac{1}{2}} = \frac{2}{26} = \frac{1}{13}.$$

The probability that a black card is a three is $\frac{1}{13}$.

There are 4 threes in the deck so

$$P(\text{three}) = \frac{4}{52} = \frac{1}{13}.$$

$$P(\text{black} \mid \text{three}) = \frac{P(\text{black and three})}{P(\text{three})} =$$

$$\frac{\frac{1}{26}}{\frac{1}{13}} = \frac{13}{26} = \frac{1}{2}.$$

The probability that a three is a black card is $\frac{1}{2}$.

The probability that a black card is a three is not the same as the probability that a three is a black card.

**Rubric**

1 point for probability that a black card is a three; 1 point for probability that a three is a black card; 1 point for stating that the probabilities are not equal

5. Landing on an odd number and landing on a prime number are not independent. The probability of landing on an odd prime number is $\frac{4}{12} = \frac{1}{3}$. The probability of landing on an odd number is $\frac{6}{12} = \frac{1}{2}$. The probability of landing on a prime number is $\frac{5}{12}$.

Two events A and B are independent if the conditional probability of A given B is equal to the probability of A and the conditional probability of B given A is equal to the probability of B.

$$P(\text{odd} \mid \text{prime}) = \frac{P(\text{odd and prime})}{P(\text{prime})} =$$

$$\frac{\frac{1}{3}}{\frac{5}{12}} = \frac{4}{5}$$

$P(\text{odd}) = \frac{1}{2}$, so $P(\text{odd} \mid \text{prime}) \neq P(\text{odd})$. Therefore, the events are not independent.

**Rubric**

1 point for answer;
2 points for explanation

6.

$$P(A \mid B) = \frac{P(A \text{ and } B)}{P(B)} = \frac{P(A) \cdot P(B)}{P(B)} = P(A)$$

$$P(B \mid A) = \frac{P(A \text{ and } B)}{P(A)} = \frac{P(A) \cdot P(B)}{P(A)} = P(B)$$

**Rubric**

2 points for showing $P(A \mid B) = P(A)$;
2 points for showing $P(B \mid A) = P(B)$

7. Since the events are independent,

$$P(\text{stars}) = \frac{P(\text{stars and purple})}{P(\text{purple})}.$$

$$P(\text{stars and purple}) = \frac{30}{60} = \frac{1}{2};$$

$$P(\text{purple}) = \frac{45}{60} = \frac{3}{4};\ P(\text{stars}) = \frac{1}{2} \div \frac{3}{4} = \frac{2}{3};$$

$\frac{2}{3} \cdot 60 = 40$, so 40 of the colored balls have stars on them.

**Rubric**

1 point for answer; 2 points for work involving conditional probability

8. Yes, buying a snack is independent of buying a regular price ticket.

The total number of tickets is $84 + 28 + 126 + 42 = 280$.

The total number of regular priced tickets is $126 + 42 = 168$.

The total number of people who bought a snack is $84 + 126 = 210$.

$$P(\text{regular price}) = \frac{168}{280} = \frac{3}{5}$$

$$P(\text{snack}) = \frac{210}{280} = \frac{3}{4}$$

$$P(\text{snack and regular price}) = \frac{126}{280} = \frac{9}{20}$$

$$P(\text{snack | regular price}) = \frac{\frac{9}{20}}{\frac{3}{5}} = \frac{3}{4}$$

$$P(\text{regular price | snack}) = \frac{\frac{9}{20}}{\frac{3}{4}} = \frac{3}{5}$$

$P(\text{snack | regular price}) = P(\text{snack})$ and $P(\text{regular price | snack}) = P(\text{regular price})$, so the events are independent.

**Rubric**

1 point for answer; 3 points for explanation involving conditional probabilities

9. There are 50 even numbers, so

$$P(A) = \frac{50}{100} = \frac{1}{2}.$$

There are 20 multiples of 5, so

$$P(B) = \frac{20}{100} = \frac{1}{5}.$$

There are 50 numbers that are greater than 50, so $P(C) = \frac{50}{100} = \frac{1}{2}.$

There are 10 even numbers that are multiples of 5, so $P(A \text{ and } B) = \frac{10}{100} = \frac{1}{10}.$

There are 25 even numbers that are greater than 50, so

$$P(A \text{ and } C) = \frac{25}{100} = \frac{1}{4}.$$

a. $P(A \mid B) = \dfrac{P(A \text{ and } B)}{P(B)} = \dfrac{\frac{1}{10}}{\frac{1}{5}} = \dfrac{1}{2}$

b. $P(B \mid A) = \dfrac{P(A \text{ and } B)}{P(A)} = \dfrac{\frac{1}{10}}{\frac{1}{2}} = \dfrac{1}{5}$

c. $P(A \mid C) = \dfrac{P(A \text{ and } C)}{P(C)} = \dfrac{\frac{1}{4}}{\frac{1}{2}} = \dfrac{1}{2}$

d. $P(C \mid A) = \dfrac{P(A \text{ and } C)}{P(A)} = \dfrac{\frac{1}{4}}{\frac{1}{2}} = \dfrac{1}{2}$

e. $P(A \mid B) = P(A)$ and $P(B \mid A) = P(B)$, so events $A$ and $B$ are independent.
$P(A \mid C) = P(A)$ and $P(C \mid A) = P(C)$, so events $A$ and $C$ are independent.

**Rubric**

a. 1 point
b. 1 point
c. 1 point
d. 1 point
e. 1 point for each answer with explanation

# S.CP.4* Answers

1. D

2. A, C, D

3. a. Not independent
   b. Independent
   c. Not independent
   d. Not independent
   e. Independent
   f. Not independent

4. a.

| | Chicken | Fish | Total |
|---|---|---|---|
| **Man** | 36 | 9 | 45 |
| **Woman** | 31 | 24 | 55 |
| **Total** | 67 | 33 | 100 |

b. $P(\text{man} \mid \text{fish}) = \dfrac{9}{33} = \dfrac{3}{11} \approx 0.27$

c. $P(\text{woman} \mid \text{chicken}) = \dfrac{31}{67} \approx 0.46$

**Rubric**
a. 3 points
b. 1 point
c. 1 point

5. a.

| | Allergy | No allergy | Total |
|---|---|---|---|
| **Positive** | 29 | 58 | 87 |
| **Negative** | 1 | 912 | 913 |
| **Total** | 30 | 970 | 1000 |

b. $P(\text{allergy} \mid \text{tests positive}) = \dfrac{29}{87} \approx 0.33$

**Rubric**
a. 2 points
b. 1 point

6. a.

| | Regular soda | Diet soda | Total |
|---|---|---|---|
| **Hamburger** | 90 | 40 | 130 |
| **Hot dog** | 70 | 50 | 120 |
| **Total** | 160 | 90 | 250 |

b. $P(\text{hamburger} \mid \text{diet soda}) = \dfrac{40}{90} = \dfrac{4}{9}$

c. $P(\text{regular soda} \mid \text{hot dog}) = \dfrac{70}{120} = \dfrac{7}{12}$

d. $P(\text{hamburger}) = \dfrac{130}{250} = \dfrac{13}{25}$

$\dfrac{4}{9} \neq \dfrac{13}{25}$, so the events are not independent.

Showing $P(\text{hamburger and diet soda}) \neq P(\text{hamburger}) \cdot P(\text{diet soda})$ is also an acceptable explanation.

e. $P(\text{regular soda}) = \dfrac{160}{250} = \dfrac{16}{25}$

$\dfrac{7}{12} \neq \dfrac{16}{25}$, so the events are not independent.

Showing $P(\text{hot dog and regular soda}) \neq P(\text{hot dog}) \cdot P(\text{regular soda})$ is also an acceptable explanation.

**Rubric**
a. 2 points
b. 1 point
c. 1 point
d. 1 point for answer;
   0.5 point for explanation
e. 1 point for answer;
   0.5 point for explanation

# S.CP.5* Answers

1. B
2. C
3. A, C, E
4. a. About 34% of the test subjects who test positive have the allergy.

   $P$(has allergy | tests positive) =
   $\frac{10}{29} \approx 0.34$

   b. About 95% of the test subjects who do not have the allergy test negative.

   $P$(tests negative | does not have allergy) $= \frac{369}{388} \approx 0.95$

   **Rubric**

   a. 1 point

   b. 1 point

5. a. $90 - 18 = 72$ trains on line A arrive on time, and $70 - 14 = 56$ trains on line B arrive on time.

   $P$(on time | line A) $= \frac{72}{90} = 0.8$, so 80% of trains on line A arrive on time.

   $P$(on time) $= \frac{72+56}{90+70} = \frac{128}{160} = 0.8$, so 80% of all trains arrive on time.

   b. Yes. The percent of trains on line A that arrive on time is the same as the percent of all trains that arrive on time. Therefore, a train being on line A and a train arriving on time are independent events.

   **Rubric**

   a. 1 point for each answer; 0.5 point for expressing each probability as a percent

   b. 1 point for concluding that the events are independent; 1 point for explanation

6. $\frac{55}{125} = 0.44 = 44\%$ of the students who play basketball also play soccer.

   **Rubric**

   1 point for answer; 1 point for work

7. a. $60 + 90 = 150$ people bought a snack. 90 of those people bought a ticket at the regular price.

   $P$(regular price | snack) $= \frac{90}{150} = 0.6$

   b. No.

   $90 + 54 = 144$ people bought a ticket at the regular price. 90 of those people bought a snack.

   $P$(snack | regular price) $= \frac{90}{144} = 0.625$

   $P$(regular price | snack) does not equal $P$(snack | regular price).

   c. 60% of the people who bought a snack bought a ticket at the regular price.

   62.5% of the people who bought a ticket at the regular price bought a snack.

   **Rubric**

   a. 1 point for answer; 1 point for work

   b. 1 point for answer; 1 point for explanation

   c. 1 point for each answer

8. a. Sylvia found the percent of students who got more than 6 hours of sleep who scored below 70% on the test, not the percent of students who scored below 70% on the test who got more than 6 hours of sleep.

   b. $P$(more than 6 hours | scored below 70%) $= \dfrac{20}{29} \approx 0.69 = 69\%$

   **Rubric**

   a. 1 point

   b. 1 point

9.

| | Mutation | No mutation | Total |
|---|---|---|---|
| **Test positive** | 19 | 49 | 68 |
| **Test negative** | 1 | 931 | 932 |
| **Total** | 20 | 980 | 1000 |

$P$(mutation | test positive) $= \dfrac{19}{68} \approx 0.28$,

so 28% of mice that test positive have the mutation.

**Rubric**

0.5 point for each cell filled in the table correctly; 1 point for using the values 19 and 68 from the table to describe the ratio; 1 point for expressing answer as a percent to the nearest unit

# S.CP.6* Answers

1. C
2. C
3. A, D, G
4. B
5. C
6. E
7. H
8.

| | Red | Black | Total |
|---|---|---|---|
| **Number** | 18 | 18 | 36 |
| **No number** | 8 | 8 | 16 |
| **Total** | 26 | 26 | 52 |

18 of the 26 red cards have a number on them. Therefore, $\frac{18}{26} = \frac{9}{13}$ of the red cards have a number on them.

18 of the 36 cards with a number on them are red. Therefore, $\frac{18}{36} = \frac{1}{2}$ of the numbered cards are red.

### Rubric

1 point for completed table; 1 point for each answer

9. a.

| | A | B | C | D | Total |
|---|---|---|---|---|---|
| **Action** | 12 | 9 | 8 | 11 | 40 |
| **Comedy** | 13 | 11 | 15 | 4 | 43 |
| **Drama** | 6 | 11 | 7 | 18 | 42 |
| **Total** | 31 | 31 | 30 | 33 | 125 |

b. Students who prefer action movies: 40
Students in block C who prefer action movies: 8

$\frac{8}{40} = \frac{1}{5}$ of the students who prefer action movies are in Ms. Peters's block C class.

c. Students in block D: 33
Students in who prefer dramas and are in block D: 18

$\frac{18}{33} = \frac{6}{11}$ of the students in Ms. Peters's block D class prefer dramas.

d. Students in block B: 31
Students who prefer comedies: 43
Students in block B who prefer comedies: 11

$\frac{11}{31}$ of the students in Ms. Peters's block B class prefer comedies, so the probability that a randomly selected student who is in Ms. Peters's block B class prefers comedies is $\frac{11}{31}$.

$\frac{11}{43}$ of the students who prefer comedies are in Ms. Peters's block B class, so the probability that a randomly selected student who prefers comedies is in Ms. Peters's block B class is $\frac{11}{43}$.

Possible answer: The two probabilities are not the same because the total number of students who prefer comedies is different from the number of students who are in Ms. Peters's block B class, even though the number of students who are in both groups is the same. The two probabilities will have the same numerator, but not the same denominator.

### Rubric

a. 0.1 point for each entry
b. 0.5 point for answer; 1 point for work
c. 0.5 point for answer; 1 point for work
d. 0.5 point for each answer; 2 points for reasonable explanation

# S.CP.7* Answers

1. B, C, D

2. D

3. C

4. a. $p = 0.5$
   b. $p > 0.5$
   c. $p < 0.5$
   d. $p < 0.5$
   e. $p > 0.5$

5. $P(\text{less than 5}) = \dfrac{4}{16}$;

   $P(\text{greater than 10}) = \dfrac{6}{16}$;

   $P(\text{less than 5 and greater than 10}) = \dfrac{0}{16}$;

   $P(\text{less than 5 or greater than 10}) = \dfrac{4}{16} + \dfrac{6}{16} = \dfrac{10}{16} = 0.625$

   **Rubric**
   1 point for answer; 2 points for work

6. $P(\text{odd}) = \dfrac{18}{36}$;

   $P(\text{less than 4}) = \dfrac{3}{36}$;

   $P(\text{odd and less than 4}) = \dfrac{2}{36}$;

   $P(\text{odd or less than 4}) = \dfrac{18}{36} + \dfrac{3}{36} - \dfrac{2}{36} = \dfrac{19}{36} \approx 0.53$

   **Rubric**
   1 point for answer; 2 points for work

7. a. Amanda forgot to subtract the probability that a randomly selected employee takes the subway and a bus.

   b. $P(\text{subway}) = \dfrac{456}{1000}$; $P(\text{bus}) = \dfrac{427}{1000}$;

   $P(\text{subway and bus}) = \dfrac{427 - 310}{1000} = \dfrac{117}{1000}$;

   $P(\text{subway or bus}) = \dfrac{456}{1000} + \dfrac{427}{1000} - \dfrac{117}{1000} = \dfrac{766}{1000} = 0.766$

   c. Possible answers:
   The probability that a randomly selected employee does not take the subway or a bus to get to work is the complement of the probability that a randomly selected employee does take the subway or a bus to get to work. So, the probability is $1 - 0.766 = 0.234$.

Completing a table can also show that 234 of the 1000 randomly selected employees do not take the subway or a bus.

|        | Subway | No subway | Total |
|--------|--------|-----------|-------|
| Bus    | 117    | 310       | 427   |
| No bus | 339    | 234       | 573   |
| Total  | 456    | 544       | 1000  |

$P(\text{no bus and no subway}) = \dfrac{234}{1000} = 0.234$

### Rubric

a. 1 point

b. 1 point for answer; 1 point for using addition rule

c. 1 point for answer; 1 point for reasoning

8. The probability is 1.

$P(\text{black}) = \dfrac{35}{100};\ P(\text{no stars}) = \dfrac{90}{100};$

$P(\text{black and no stars}) = \dfrac{25}{100};$

$P(\text{black or no stars}) = \dfrac{35}{100} + \dfrac{90}{100} - \dfrac{25}{100} = \dfrac{100}{100} = 1$

Any randomly selected ball will either be black or not have stars on it.

### Rubric

1 point for answer; 1 point for justification

9. a. $P(\text{senior}) = \dfrac{4022}{16{,}112};\ P(\text{female}) = \dfrac{9184}{16{,}112};$

$P(\text{senior and female}) = \dfrac{2296}{16{,}112};$

$P(\text{senior or female}) = \dfrac{4022}{16{,}112} + \dfrac{9184}{16{,}112} - \dfrac{2296}{16{,}112} = \dfrac{10{,}910}{16{,}112} \approx 0.68$

b. $P(\text{junior}) = \dfrac{4100}{16{,}112};\ P(\text{male}) = \dfrac{6928}{16{,}112};$

$P(\text{junior and male}) = \dfrac{1750}{16{,}112};$

$P(\text{junior or male}) = \dfrac{4100}{16{,}112} + \dfrac{6928}{16{,}112} - \dfrac{1750}{16{,}112} = \dfrac{9278}{16{,}112} \approx 0.58$

c. It is more likely that a randomly selected student is a senior or female, because $0.68 > 0.58$.

### Rubric

a. 1 point for answer; 1 point for work using addition property

b. 1 point for answer; 1 point for work using addition property

c. 1 point for answer; 1 point for explanation

# S.MD.6(+)* Answers

1. C
2. B
3. A, C, D
4. If the game is fair, the probability of winning is $\frac{1}{6}$ for each player. The probability of not winning is $1 - \frac{1}{6} = \frac{5}{6}$. The probability of not winning 7 games in a row is $\left(\frac{5}{6}\right)^7 \approx 0.279 = 27.9\%$.

**Rubric**
2 points

5. The table shows the possible sums.

|   | 1 | 2 | 3 | 4 | 5 | 6 |
|---|---|---|---|---|---|---|
| 1 | 2 | 3 | 4 | 5 | 6 | 7 |
| 2 | 3 | 4 | 5 | 6 | 7 | 8 |
| 3 | 4 | 5 | 6 | 7 | 8 | 9 |
| 4 | 5 | 6 | 7 | 8 | 9 | 10 |

There are 6 outcomes with sums of 2, 6, or 10.

There are 6 outcomes with sums of 3 or 5.

There are 6 outcomes with sums of 4 or 8.

There are 6 other outcomes: sums of 7 or 9.

Since each player has an equal chance of winning, the game is fair.

**Rubric**
1 point for answer; 2 points for explanation

6. The table shows the possible sums.

|   | 1 | 2 | 3 | 4 |
|---|---|---|---|---|
| 1 | 2 | 3 | 4 | 5 |
| 2 | 3 | 4 | 5 | 6 |
| 3 | 4 | 5 | 6 | 7 |
| 4 | 5 | 6 | 7 | 8 |

There are 16 outcomes with 8 even sums and 8 odd sums. The game is fair because each player has an equal chance of winning.

Possible answers:

Player A wins if the sum is 2, 4, or 5, and player B wins if the sum is 3, 6, 7, or 8.

Player A wins if the sum is less than 5, and player B wins if the sum is greater than 5. If the sum is 5, the players spin again.

**Rubric**
2 points for showing the game is fair; 2 points for describing another fair game

7. a. Of the students in the class, $\frac{2}{5}$ prefer the science museum and $\frac{3}{5}$ prefer the nature center.

b. Of the students in row 1, $\frac{5}{6}$ prefer the science museum and $\frac{1}{6}$ prefer the nature center.

c. Of the students in the random sample, $\frac{1}{6}$ prefer the science museum and $\frac{5}{6}$ prefer the nature center.

d. The census in part a is the most fair method of deciding the destination because each student has the opportunity to express his or her preference. The random sample in part c is the next most fair method because each student has an equal probability of being able to express his or her preference. The convenience sample in part b is the least fair method because only the students in row 1 have the opportunity to express their preference.

## Rubric

a. 0.5 point for each proportion
b. 0.5 point for each proportion
c. 0.5 point for each proportion
d. 1 point for correct ranking; 2 points for valid explanations

8. a. Each player could get 2 more points and then the next toss would result in one of the players winning, so the maximum number of tosses needed to finish the game is 5.

   Using H for heads and T for tails, the possible outcomes for 5 tosses are HHHHH, THHHH, HTHHH, HHTHH, HHHTH, HHHHT, TTHHH, THTHH, THHTH, THHHT, HTTHH, HTHTH, HTHHT, HHTTH, HHTHT, HHHTT, TTTHH, TTHTH, TTHHT, THTTH, THTHT, THHTT, HTTTH, HTTHT, HTHTT, HHTTT, TTTTH, TTTHT, TTHTT, THTTT, HTTTT, and TTTTT.

   b. Stephan needs 3 more points to win, so he would win if at least 3 heads result. There are 16 such outcomes. Nariam also needs 3 more points to win, so she would win if at least 3 tails result. There are 16 such outcomes.

   c. The total number of possible outcomes is 32. The probability that Stephan would have won is $\frac{16}{32} = 0.5$, and the probability that Nariam would have won is $\frac{16}{32} = 0.5$. Since each player had an equal chance of winning, deciding to evenly divide the jelly beans is fair.

## Rubric

a. 1 point for maximum number of tosses; 2 points for sample space
b. 1 point for each answer
c. 1 point

# S.MD.7(+)* Answers

1. D

2. B, C, E, F

3. Consider the probabilities of undesirable outcomes:

   - For those who get the vaccine, there is a 5% probability of getting the disease and a 2% chance of having an allergic reaction. If these events are mutually exclusive, the probability of one of these outcomes is 7%. If the events are not mutually exclusive, the probability is greater than 5%, but less than 7%.

   - For those who do not get the vaccine, there is a 10% probability of getting the disease.

   It is better to risk the vaccine since the probability of an undesirable outcome is less.

   **Rubric**

   3 points

4. If the coach leaves the goaltender in the game, the road team has a $\frac{1}{28.6} \approx 3.5\%$ probability of scoring a goal. If the coach replaces the goaltender, the road team has a $\frac{1375}{10,000} \approx 13.75\%$ probability of scoring a goal.

   The road team coach should replace the goaltender with another offensive player to maximize the probability that the road team scores a goal.

   **Rubric**

   3 points

5. a. Assume a population of 100,000 people, and complete a two-way frequency table for each test.

   Test A:

   |  | Tests positive | Tests negative | Total |
   |---|---|---|---|
   | Has virus | 485 | 15 | 500 |
   | No virus | 2985 | 96,515 | 99,500 |
   | Total | 3470 | 96,530 | 100,000 |

   $$P(\text{no virus} \mid \text{tests positive}) = \frac{2985}{3470}$$
   $$\approx 86\%$$

   Test B:

   |  | Tests positive | Tests negative | Total |
   |---|---|---|---|
   | Has virus | 495 | 5 | 500 |
   | No virus | 4975 | 94,525 | 99,500 |
   | Total | 5470 | 94,530 | 100,000 |

   $$P(\text{no virus} \mid \text{tests positive}) = \frac{4975}{5470}$$
   $$\approx 91\%$$

   b. Use the tables from part a.

   Test A:

   $$P(\text{has virus} \mid \text{tests neg.}) = \frac{15}{96,530}$$
   $$\approx 0.016\%$$

   Test B:

   $$P(\text{has virus} \mid \text{tests neg.}) = \frac{5}{94,530}$$
   $$\approx 0.005\%$$

   c. If the virus is very contagious, the better test is less likely to identify someone who actually has the virus as not having the virus. Since 0.005% < 0.016%, test B would be better.

d. If the side effects of the medicine used to fight the virus are substantial, the better test is less likely to identify someone who doesn't have the virus as having the virus. Since 86% < 91%, test A would be better.

**Rubric**
2 points for each part

6. Assume a population of 10,000 parts, and complete a two-way frequency table as shown.

|       | Not defective | Defective | Total  |
|-------|---------------|-----------|--------|
| A     | 1940          | 60        | 2000   |
| B     | 2925          | 75        | 3000   |
| C     | 4950          | 50        | 5000   |
| Total | 9815          | 185       | 10,000 |

Calculate the probability that a defective part is from each supplier.

$$P(\text{defective part from A}) = \frac{60}{185} \approx 0.324$$

$$P(\text{defective part from B}) = \frac{75}{185} \approx 0.405$$

$$P(\text{defective part from C}) = \frac{50}{185} \approx 0.270$$

Since the probability is greatest for supplier B, that supplier is most likely responsible for the defective part.

**Rubric**
3 points for determining the probabilities;
1 point for determining the supplier with the greatest probability;
1 point for answering the question